9728
V726
1995

D0949587

WALKING TO
LA MILPA

LIVING IN GUATEMALA WITH ARMIES,
DEMONS, ABRAZOS, AND DEATH

ALSO BY THE AUTHOR:

A FIRE IN THE EARTH

WALKING TO
LA MILPA

LIVING IN GUATEMALA WITH ARMIES,
DEMONS, ABRAZOS, AND DEATH

BY MARCOS MCPEEK VILLATORO

Moyer Bell
Wakefield, Rhode Island & London

Published by Moyer Bell

First Edition

**LIBRARY OF CONGRESS
CATALOGING-IN-PUBLICATION DATA**

Villatoro, Marcos McPeek.
Walking to La Milpa : living in
Guatemala with armies, demons, abrazos,
and death / Marcos McPeek Villatoro.— 1st. ed.
        p.   cm.

   1. Guatemala — Description and
travel. 2. Villatoro, Marcos
McPeek — Journeys — Guatemala.
I. Title.
F1464.3.V55   1996
917.28104′53 — dc20   95-45126
                                        CIP

   ISBN 1-55921-164-4   (alk. paper)

Printed in the United States of America.
Distributed in North America by Publishers Group West,
P.O. Box 8843, Emeryville, CA 94662,
800-788-3123 (in California 510-658-3453)

PARA MICHELLE, POR SUPUESTO

CONTENTS

WALKING TO LA MILPA

LIVING IN GUATEMALA WITH ARMIES, DEMONS, ABRAZOS, AND DEATH

PROLOGUE

A handful of decades ago in a small town in El Salvador, my mother, Amanda del Carmen, then five years old, looked up and saw her grandfather rush into the room. "*Vámonos cipotes, vámonos!*" don Hipólito shooed them with a loud, nervous whisper. "Let's go kids, let's go." They moved toward the back door. Her mother had a sick baby—my uncle—in her arms. They rushed out back, just as machetes banged against the front door. My family hid out in *la milpa* all night long. The baby, feverish with pneumonia, died that night among the cornstalks. There was no time for mourning once the shooting began. Bullets rang through the streets of their little town with machine-gun laughter.

The rest of my mother's memories are visions broken by shrapnel. She still can see an old man with a donkey-drawn cart, who hid them in his dilapidated vehicle and carried them away. Down the dirt road someone held a lantern, beckoning my family through the night and toward a vague safety.

These are the fragmented memories of a child witnessing the incipient moments of the 1932 *Matanza*, The Massacre. In one evening Amanda del Carmen captured the total tragedy of her mother country: Poverty that rises from suffering, and an army that will stand for no restlessness. An endeavored revolution had begun that evening, led by a handful of ideologists and several hundred campesinos who had only machetes and constant hunger as their weapons. They beat their anger and dire hope for change against my grandfather's door. Don Hipólito was one of the few local middle class, and the nearest target for a desperate people. Everyone was afraid, knowing an uprising seemed imminent.

In the days following another ubiquitous fear would take control, led by General Maximiliano Hernández Martínez. Though he was the President of El Salvador, the man was better known as *El Brujo*, The Warlock.

History snatches up the unraveled strings of my mother's memory. General Martinez had ordered a *limpieza*, a cleaning of the land, ridding it of any trace of communism. He gave the command to kill anyone who held a machete. Though used as a limited weapon in the failed revolt, in Central America a machete is a farmer's hoe, his axe, a work tool. Every poor man carries one as an extension of his arm.

Stories quickly gathered in the minds of survivors.* A line of 250 men were given shovels and told to start digging. As they worked on the long trench that was to be their common

---

*Many of these stories and other details of the 1932 massacre can be found in *Matanza*, which is seen as the standard reference for the events leading up to the mass killings. *Matanza*, Thomas P. Anderson, Curbstone Press, 1992.

sepulcher, soldiers just behind them crawled over a jeep and assembled a machine gun. Other soldiers handed farmers string to tie one another together by the thumbs. The jeep moved to one end of the line, then drove just behind the men as one soldier kept the gun beaded on their backs and watched the line fall like dominoes into the grave.

Five days into *la limpieza*, the government bequeathed to the population a chance to prove that they were not with the subversives. They were told to go to a certain office building to take a card which verified that the receiver was not a communist.

People in panic began lining up in front of these buildings, almost fighting one another to get in. The gun-mounted jeep waited until the line reached around the corner to the end of the street before it drove down the road and aimed at the people. Their screams dropped to the ground.

Now he felt that communism (or better said, the communists) had been liquidated in his country. *El Brujo* had photos taken of the piles of the 30,000 dead. He had them made into postcards, and sent them out to the various people with *Felíz Matanza* written on the back. Happy Massacre.

My mother's memory begins and ends quickly that evening sixty years ago. She and my grandmother have told these and other stories. I have snatched them up like clods of rich soil around hidden roots.

My mother brought me into the world via San Francisco, California. After living several years of childhood there, we moved to my father's home in East Tennessee. Such a move could have been a clean cut through the umbilical cord that connected me back to the Old Country. My mother made sure that did not happen.

While living in East Tennessee I saw El Salvador through my mother's skin, her hair, her phenotypic mestizoness (mixed facial features of Nahuatl and Mayan with blood of the Spaniards). The food she prepared for us spoke of a distant country. Rarely did a day pass that we did not eat tortillas. My father complied with Mom's wishes and built the interior of our home with colonial-shaped arches. Through my eyes East Tennessee Appalachian and Central American Salvadoran were not a strange mix at all. They were completely ordinary, as everyday as sausage gravy and grits with tortillas and jalapeños.

She made sure the culture remained alive. Yet she did not care to speak about those other memories, ones fragmented by the bloodletting whim of a Warlock. I had to learn about those events on my own. Only after I moved to Central America did Mom open herself to the shrapnelled memories of a distant childhood.

In my early twenties my Latino family met in Mexico City to spend a Christmas together. It was then that I became enamored with my hispanic heritage. Though I understood some Spanish, my abilities in the language had turned torpid after living much of my youth in a monolingual (i.e., English only) environment. After that Christmas I asked my mother to speak to me only in Spanish. I memorized lists, learning fifty new words a day. I worked through the past perfect subjunctive until it leapt in my brain like a horse over etymological fences. I read everything Gabriel García Márquez and Pablo Neruda wrote.

All this naturally led to a return to the "Motherland." My wife Michelle had the idea of doing some type of community work overseas. I just wanted to get to Central America. We moved to Nicaragua in the mid-eighties with a group called Witness for Peace, which allowed us to live in a war zone for almost a year. That year shook up any youthful ideals that we had harbored. I remember, after a month of collecting affidavits on Contra war atrocities (the "norms" of war: burned villages, raped women, kidnapped men and slit throats), having difficulties sleeping at night. One afternoon a zealous, drunk Sandinista youth aimed a loaded M-16 at Michelle and me. "Let me show you what my father did to the gringos with their own guns," he slurred. As I rattled off a reason to not kill gringos today, as it could harm their revolutionary endeavors, his mother jumped toward him and snapped the long, rectangular cartridge from the automatic. She hid it in her dress and smiled, obviously embarrassed.

When we returned to the States, I began washing my hands every half hour. I dreamed of mad dogs and death by rabies. I still could not sleep. A psychologist friend presumed it to be posttraumatic stress, and likened it to the syndrome that many Vietnam War Vets have suffered.

Such incidents and the need for mental convalescence kept us at home for a couple of years. Still, the time in Nicaragua had not done away with our desires to return to Central America. I am not sure why we went back. Michelle still had the desire to work among the poor; I suppose I felt that I had left personal, unfinished business back in the "Old Country."

We jumped aboard a missionary ship.* This seemed to fit both of our agendas. In Nicaragua our job took us to several areas in the war zones. Through mission work we could remain in one town and become part of one community.

Christian missioners have been put on a critical and historical chopping block in recent years. In bringing their evangelical zeal to poor countries, as well as their perspective on rousing up peace and justice in poor nations, many missioners have also broken down the cultural strengths of indigenous peoples. Anyone who joins such a group is becoming part of the destruction.

Missioners, like all entities that come from the outside of poor countries, have two things that the vast majority of the local population does not have: money and power. No matter how much they cling to a belief or cause, those two resources will stand as walls between the missioners and the people being missioned to. Sometimes, however, such power can be used for the good of many. In the end, much depends upon each individual's relationship to local people, as well as to how they decide to wield the power bequeathed them. Such decisions made by missioners or anyone else who holds power and yet wishes to make friends with poor and suffering people is what I term "Walking to *La Milpa*."

Being a Latino is no quick ticket into any Spanish speaking community. Much like in Nicaragua, as a U.S. citizen I quickly learned that I was just another gringo who had come

---

*Michelle and I were privileged to work with one of the more renowned institutions called the Maryknoll Lay Missioners. This group, an offshoot of the Maryknoll Priests, Brothers, and Sisters, has missioners throughout the world. Maryknoll itself is almost as old as this century, having at first sent priests to China, then in the 1940s, expanding into Latin America.

into town. Just like any other missioner, I too had to learn how to walk to La Milpa. I also learned that one does not walk alone. An indigenous hand must lead you there.

La Milpa is a term used specifically in Central America to say cornfield. Yet to translate the word without a sense of history and mythology is to lose the value of the term itself. Corn is a sacred food in Central American countries. It, along with beans and rice, is the main source of survival. I have watched poor farmers gather around a small wooden table and consume dozens of tortillas in short order. They scoop up their beans, rice, and occasional chicken into the curve of the flat corn and adroitly bring it to their mouths without missing a drop.

The articulation of corn-as-sacred is best seen in Guatemala. The indigenous people of that country are known as *Hombres de Maíz*, The Corn Men. In the vision of the Mayas, human flesh was made from maize dough. The corn plant itself is a demonstration of harmony between humans and the earth. The Mayas see corn as the sustenance of life as well as a plant that cannot seed itself without the intervention of humans. The two need each other in order to survive.*

*Numerous books have been written on the history and beliefs of the Maya people. I suggest that any book written by Linda Schele should be read in order to reach a deeper and more thorough understanding of the ancient Mayan world. The information on the value of corn mentioned above is taken from *A Forest of Kings, the Untold Story of the Ancient Maya* by Linda Schele and David Freidel, 1990, William Morrow and Company, Inc., New York, p. 243. Copyright Linda Schele and David Freidel.

To walk to la milpa is to be invited into another people's sense of the sacred. I did not understand this at first. Cornfields have never said very much to me in philosophical or spiritual terms. My only experience of corn was driving by miles of midwest fields, staring at the millions of rows that would be collected as cattle feed. I quickly learned that the small plot of land that a man depended upon to feed his family and thus survive the next season stood lifetimes away from the fattening produce raised in the Iowa hills. I also learned how painful it can be to walk into someone's milpa. Living in a world that was not my own meant letting go of the desire to control (not one of my best qualities). It also meant trusting the folks who had invited me into their cornfield. As they held their hand out to me and gently guided me into their crop, much like teaching a baby how to walk, I began to see that the cornfield was not necessarily frightening. It was, in fact, familiar. In walking around the countryside of Guatemala, I began to recognize the ghosts of my mother's life that she had left behind decades ago.

This book is a collection of stories that happened along the way to la milpa. My wife and I lived in Guatemala from 1989–1991. We resided in a small, jungle town of the Petén region. The name of the town is *Poptún*, which is an ancient Maya word that means either hats of stone or straw mat of stone, depending upon who you're talking with.

Poptún held no dearth of stories. I heard many tales that echoed the Latino women and men of my family, everything from military repression to the arrival of *La Ciguanaba*, the

Queen Mama of Badness, who tears the entrails out of sexually abusive men. These were not stories merely told, but lived out in the day's existence. Through the invitation of local Guatemalans who offered me friendship, I came closer to tales that my mother had lived through. I felt myself stumbling to the same cornfield that my mother and her family had hidden in during the first night of the matanza. In some ways, I have never been more afraid than when I lived in Guatemala. In the same breath I must confess that I have never felt more welcome and friendship than when residing in that country.

It has taken a few years of distance to arrive at the writing of this book. Sometimes distance is necessary so as to be kind to the tale. The joy of a wedding or the sorrow of a funeral can take on depth with time. So it has been with Guatemala. I could never look upon that country with James Joyce's attitude of staring down from the clouds while filing my fingernails. Yet I have had to walk away from that nation and its history—then from my own history within its story—for awhile. Otherwise the telling of this tale proved impossible. Sometimes the ironies that surrounded us, ones that the Guatemalan people lived with all their lives, tended to swallow our psyches. Death and Life both whipped the streets with a laughter and a cry, like a crazed couple heading for a wedding in the cemetery. Yet such ironies were normal. It has taken time to articulate such normalcy, and recognize its familiarity.

Entering into my mother's cornfield, I was lead back out by that same little girl who survived the killings. My mother later told me what was to be the ironic end of that story from her childhood. It was an ending that, only after having lived in Central America, I would fully appreciate.

A few years after La Matanza, Mom attended a Catholic high school in San Salvador. One day another girl two years younger than my mother was to go to her uncle's house for afternoon coffee. The high school's chaperon was sick. The nuns asked my mother to accompany the girl.

A large car parked in front of the Catholic school. Mom and the girl got in and were taken away. They pulled up to a large palace. As the girl wandered from room to room like she owned the place, my mother stared in awe at the opulent furniture and large rooms and the marble floor that made her heels click. Coffee was served with little sweet cakes. As they ate and talked like teenagers, General Maximiliano Hernández Martínez walked into the room. *El Brujo*, my mother said in her mind. She dared not speak that nickname.

The other girl said, "Amandita, I would like you to meet my uncle."

Mom stared into the eyes of *El Brujo*, who took her hand and greeted her. He smiled. "So very good to have you in my presence, Amanda del Carmen."

He joined them for coffee and was the most perfect gentleman.

CHAPTER ONE

WALKING AROUND

You would believe that Poptún is flat. Looking around at all the rolling hills that surround us, you'd turn from your dusty, omniscient position on the outskirts and say, "Yes. Definitely a very flat town." Except for the huge knoll just in the middle, which sticks out of the earth like some cat playing underneath a rug, this isolated little community looks pretty even.

But it's not. Whenever they placed Poptún upon the earth, a cola bottle top must have gotten caught underneath the southeast side, putting the town on the slightest tilt. I know this because of our bicycle. Michelle and I live near that southeast corner, close to the army's runway. Whenever I ride my bike to the parish or any other place on the northwest end, I can practically coast from my door all the way to my destination. It's a slow coast, one that asks for half a pedal of power from time to time.

To return home I must put an even, consistent pressure upon the chain. I enter the house slightly sweaty, with clean wind in my lungs. On hot, dry April days I wonder if it's not a good idea to go to the southeast corner, lift it up, look for that cola top, and pitch it to one side.

We own a grey Shimano twelve-speed top-line mountain terrain-tread bicycle. We also have a brown Nissan Patrol four-wheel drive Jeep (1985, with 76,000 kilometers), but it's in the shop with a busted steering column. A replacement part won't be coming in until next week. The Shimano gets us around these days. As we have only one, Michelle and I take turns. I once tried to talk Michelle into riding together on the bike like most young fellows do, with their lovely girlfriends perched on top of the handlebars or the base bar like a parrot while they pedal around town. To me nothing seemed more romantic.

"There's nothing romantic about having a thin steel bar biting into your butt," said Michelle.

"I don't see any of those girls complaining about pain."

"It's new love. You don't complain about anything."

"Come on honey, it looks like fun."

"Okay then. But you sit on the bar. I'll take the seat and pedal."

This discussion died quickly. I proposed that we bike alone until the car was out of the shop.

It's not such a problem to wait. We use the jeep mostly to visit outlying villages or to carry equipment. But it's good to leave the car behind whenever possible. Ours is one of the few vehicles on these roads. None of the local people we work with own one. Since the town is almost perfectly flat, bicycles are the norm. Besides, the thin walls of the jeep create a chasm between you and those who walk around. The possibilities for visiting on the streets from a car are nil. Who has time to visit while driving? The only thought in mind as you push into second gear is your destination, not the path that takes you to it.

Bicycling is different. There are no walls between you and the people walking about. As you coast by you wave, wish a good day, or slow to a stop and talk.

Take for example doña Anita. That elderly woman walks at a good clip toward you, her hands balled up to her sides for equilibrium, her mouth pulled tight in concentration. Doña Anita probably isn't a day under 147 years old. A year ago we all thought she was dying of uterine cancer. In the past twelve months she's passed in and out of two comas. Each time the family prepared itself for a funeral. They bought a coffin, whispering to folks in the neighborhood that sadly, tomorrow night, rosary and wake, be there, we'll serve tamales and chocolates afterwards. About that moment she suddenly sat up in bed and blinked her eyes, complaining nothing of the cancer in her uterus but asking her daughter-in-law for beans with lots of pepper.

When approaching her on a bicycle you don't need to touch your brakes, for doña Anita snatches the handlebars and stops you in mid-flight. Before you fly over the front tire she's caught you around the neck with her bony arms, hugging you and gumming words into your ear about how wonderful the folks in town have been to help her, and how great it is to have another day of life, thanks be to God.

Ours is undoubtedly one of the better bikes in town. Few of the local folks have a Shimano 12-speed with mountain tread. Most own an amalgam of bicycles, parts collected here and there, a chain from a two-speeder, a handlebar from a rusting Schwinn. Most bikes I see don't have pedals. Riders wrap their inner arch around the tiny, middle poles like standing on a ladder rung. And air in the tires? Please, let's be realistic. Whenever we attend community meetings, the legion of bicycles leans up against one another toward the building's wall like a dozen horses in a grade-B cowboy movie. Inside at least a dozen farmers lean against the wall while we play guitar and sing songs, waiting for everyone to arrive. Portable tire pumps stick out of their back pockets like metal slingshots.

Yesterday don Chico Guzmán visited us. Chico is undoubtedly our closest friend in Poptún. Forty-four years old, a catechist (i.e., a Catholic lay preacher, also a community organizer), pure campesino, father of six. His wife died of breast cancer the year before last. He pulled up to our house on his son's rattling one-speeder and leaned it against the orange tree. I noticed that his sinewy frame was shaking slightly, and his thick, curly nest of hair quivered.

"You all right?" I asked.

"Ay don Marcos, you won't believe what just happened. This guy's heading straight toward me, and it's just getting dark. We're in Porvenir, and you know there's no electricity in that neighborhood. I swerve to avoid him, and wouldn't you know it he swerves at the exact same time toward the exact same place! Well, I picked myself off the ground, dusted off, checked to see if anything was broken or bleeding, and I look over at the guy, his legs still in the air and his head in the spokes. I offer him a hand and say, 'Hey buddy, looks like we had the same idea,' and he grumbles, 'Don't buddy me you son of a bitch.' Well, I'm not waiting around. While he's untying himself from the spokes, I'm already a good piece down the road. You've got to be careful, you know. Better to walk away from an angry man."

He came in. We made a pot of coffee, and the three of us sat down. Michelle handed him a cup. We spent the next couple of hours talking about dreams and reality, the poverty in this town, and how the community can respond to it.

Chico looked like he was on fire with hope. He's as poor as the next campesino, but his eyes burned through his lean, dark skin as he spoke of projects and ideas, of chicken cooperatives in order to sell eggs, of teaching the people to work together. The coffee tasted richer, stirred with such conversation.

I took our Shimano to don Rubén, one of the several bicycle specialists in town. I walked into his shop and sat down on a stool at his invitation. You don't just leave your bike and tell him what's the matter, and expect he can have it fixed by this afternoon. Such discourtesy is met with a, "Sorry, can't do it today." Besides, there's always time to talk.

Rubén was crouched over, dismantling the metallic intestinal tract of another Shimano similar to mine. A smaller man with a wiry, agile frame, his sleepy eyes peered patiently beyond the sprockets and into the wound. He pulled out the shattered ball bearings and held them in his greased palm like a set of gritty pearls. "There's the problem all right. Even a Shimano can't withstand the Poptún roads forever. No air in his tires, no wonder he lost the bearings. Nothing to absorb the shock. You should always carry a tire pump around. You never know."

After we chatted awhile, I showed him my beast. The brakes needed to be straightened, as they were rubbing against the tire itself. The chain, easily seen, was caked with a few months of muddy road (Rubén eyed the chain with a look of incredulity, as if to think, *Doesn't this gringo have any compassion for his vehicle?*). Also, there was something loose in the pedals, like a gravel bouncing around inside.

"And one final problem, don Rubén. What can you do about this brown strip down my back?" I turned around so he could see.

"Oh yeah. A common Shimano problem. Best bike in town, but they don't come with mud fenders. Either get fenders, or don't ride around in the rain."

He told me it would be ready by tomorrow. I thanked him and headed toward the door. He also came out to take a break, and to continue chatting with the gringo. Eight bicycles rattled back and forth as we spoke. "Poptún is made for bikes." He leaned against the door and crossed his arms. A tiny crescent wrench stuck upward from his closed fingers like an antenna. "The town is almost perfectly flat. But not quite. The southeast end—you know, where you live?—it's up slightly higher. Just barely. This town is tilted. Nobody believes me. But I've ridden bikes on these roads for too many years. There's a slant, sure enough."

I wondered if he saw my excitement, as I knew exactly what he was talking about. I wanted to share with him my cola-top theory. But I stayed quiet, knowing that I had yet to find hard facts.

The conversation continued for a good while before we shook hands goodbye. He offered me his wrist in true Guatemalan courtesy, not wanting to stain my fingers with his work day.

I left. I stood on the street. The jeep was in the shop, the bike with Rubén. I had to walk home.

It had been awhile. You get used to having wheels, whether they come in sets of four or two. Stepping out of Rubén's shop, I passed into yet another world of Poptún. I heard my name called out more, *Don Marcos, how's it going? Don Marcos, good to see you.* Between the bike shop and our home the road stretched longer, not just for walking, but for the handful of conversations along the way. This is Michelle's preferred transportation, and I see why. You learn more about town while on foot. You can't escape conversations by gearing into third or pedaling slightly faster. Everybody's equal here, even though you wear Birkenstock sandals while doña Inéz walks on sixty-year-old callouses, thick and pliable as soft leather.

Doña Inéz is pure Kekchi Indian and hardly speaks a word of Spanish. She was one of many who I ran into on the way home. Somehow we communicated, laughing as she insisted that I speak her language. I always feel like doña Inéz is flirting with me. She held my arm and patted my shoulder, grinned and gave me a sly eye, while neither of us knew what the hell the other was saying. "She's not flirting," Michelle once told me. "She treats me like that all the time too. She's just full of love."

I smiled toward the road, and below doña Inéz's indigenous, multi-green dress that wrapped around her waist half a dozen times, I saw her bare feet, hardened with the long road of life. When we parted, she smiled a toothless grin, and I saw in her eyes a beautiful woman who has dared to love life, and who silently reminded me, *Good to see you walking around, don Gringo.*

CHAPTER TWO

NEIGHBORS

Chamba, a young gentleman who is the local priest, has made a point of orienting us to his land. He took us around to meet the neighbors. We drove in his truck to the edge of town, where the dusty military airstrip stretched for two miles. Just on the other side of the runway lived an elderly couple named don Lolo and doña Roberta.

They blessed us from the moment we came in until our departure. They have a prayer altar in the middle of their bedroom, with Mary standing over it in her Guadalupe form, herself larger than the crucifix that hung to one side. The couple carefully knelt down upon the cement floor and fervently muttered through half-cleaved Our Fathers and Hail Marys, adding their own spontaneous endings that had turned orthodox through decades of prayer. Father Chamba gave them communion. They resumed their litany for several minutes afterwards.

Don Lolo snuffed the candles and meandered out to cut down a sugarcane stick for the good Padre.

"Hey don Lolo, what's your secret to long life?" asked Chamba.

"Don't stop moving. And go deaf so you don't have to listen to her," Lolo smiled as he turned his head toward his wife. Roberta was talking with Michelle, telling a story about her son in the States. Chamba laughed as he spat out sugarcane pieces.

Afterwards we drove to a *finca*, where Chamba wanted to buy fresh eggs. "I think you'll find this farm interesting," he smiled.

We passed a sign that said *Ixobel*. As Chamba geared down one of the little hills, I saw two white people walking through the woods. Soon Chamba pulled the truck up to a cabin full of Caucasians.

It was a tourist farm. People from Europe and the States walked about. Many of them smoked. They were dressed in a peculiar, bohemian fashion: no bras, few shirts for the men, wire-framed glasses, and either long hair or bald. Most were young. All of them were very white, except for the red blistering over their shoulders. Chamba explained, "They are on their way to Tikal. Our pyramids that are up north."

It seemed strange to be on a part of the earth where dark brown, indigenous men and women predominate, and then to suddenly come across a corner of gringos.

Heading home, Chamba plugged a cassette of Nashville country music into his truck player. "A little sentimental touch. I beg of you, no weeping." He laughed. He loves country and bluegrass, something that I have not been particularly attracted to until now. Suddenly, however, I felt the root of the music.

Once again, two cultures wound around each other, but did not join or blend. In such moments I don't know where I am or what language to speak. Kenny Rogers sang passionately through a Guatemalan jungle. Chamba sang along, muttering through the refrain that he has heard countless times in the song "The Gambler." He asked, "What does it mean, 'to hold 'em and to fold 'em?'" I told him I'm not really sure, but I commended him on his English.

Chamba took us to the ruins of Tikal. We followed the routes of all those tourists who have passed through the jungle, who now walk around like ants over a dead person, climbing the stony bones of the cadaver.

The site was tremendous to see for the first time. Great stone structures rise far above the treetops of the jungle. Here, in this national park, the jungle had not been cut back, but was thick, much like you'd see in some Tarzan movie. The only paved road in the whole state of the Petén stretches from the small airport in Flores to the ruins. The rest of the roads in the *departamento* are rock, sand, and dirt. If you flew in from Guatemala City to visit the ruins, then left by plane, you'd never know that poverty existed in the Petén. You'd barely know that people's homes were here.

I felt a certain shame, that of being a clumsy gringo, tripping over another's hallowed ground.

Chamba seemed right at home. He walked up the shattered stone of one pyramid as if climbing the stairs of a house. "Come on up."

I did, but had to crawl on my belly and snatch at the steps with my hands.

Chamba looked down at me. "You all right?"

"Yeah," my voice squeaked.

"Don't be nervous. I'll get us up and back. Trust me. Only two gringos have died from falling off these steps. And that was last year."

"No more statistics, please."

We made it to the top. While Chamba perched on the edge of the top wall, looking out and breathing in the warm jungle air, I clambered into the deepest corner of the inner room atop the pyramid. From there I looked at Chamba's back and shoulders. He turned his head from side to side to take in the full view of the silenced kingdom.

Inside the room the air stood moist and cool. I looked around, as if to find the blood of sacrificed men on the walls. Nothing, except for some English graffiti on one side.

I realized I knew nothing of Maya culture. Yet this culture was the one that my mother always so proudly connected herself to. Looking at the remnants of Tikal, it was obvious that they were a tremendous civilization. I said this to Chamba. He turned from his perch and looked at me in the corner. "Not that they *were*. We *are*."

I am sure I looked at him puzzled, for he then spelled it out to me. "Archaeologists and historians and every other asshole who has come here to pick away at this place has said that the 'dead Maya civilization' used to be a great and advanced people. The presupposition is mistaken: the Mayas are not dead. We are very much alive."

I looked at him. In my dense, mestizo head, it clicked.

Chamba was Q'achiq'el Indian. His people are from the southern region of the country. He was very dark skinned, with facial features that distinguished him from any mixed blood ladino, or someone who has Spanish-European ancestry. I had to question why this did not register with me earlier. Perhaps it was because of his occupation as a Roman Catholic priest. I had immediately seen him from a European perspective, a Western mode of thinking, the traps of Christendom. Though trained by the Church, somehow he had not fallen into the same traps.

We recently met a woman named Bertila. She was forty years and sixteen pregnancies old. Due to high blood pressure, ten of those were miscarriages. We met her as she scrubbed laundry in the creek, her arms stretched a belly away from the rock. Her six children splashed about the rooted veins that wrapped around her legs.

We talked for awhile as she took a break from beating the clothes. When we asked about the birth, she offered all she knew, *Primero Dios*. It seemed her destiny, to smile that toothless innocence and say, "Whatever God wills."

Two days later she went into labor. We ran into her that night in front of the Poptún marketplace. She was walking toward the hospital, right after going to mass. "The pain comes pretty regularly now," she said, her voice trembling through a smile. We offered to get our Jeep and drive her there, but she laughed as she pointed down the road, telling us how close she was to the delivery room. She left us and walked to the hospital, about a mile away.

Two hours later she gave birth to a *leñador*, a "Wood-cutter." The boy slashed at his new life with arms that trembled toward security.

Down the street other movements were born. Raised machetes stained the moon with a splash of crimson.

As Bertila turned that night to give her new boy mother's milk, she glanced over and saw in the corner of the same room what once was a man. His eyes stared through a Picasso-chopped face while the nurses whispered outside, "They said it was soldiers."

The new Woodcutter found the nipple and stopped crying. Bertila covered his little face with her shirt, as if to save him from the breathing cadaver in the hallway. She stared down at her little man, wishing him a welcome into a less-than-innocent world.

Doña Bertila's husband, don Santiago, stopped Michelle and me yesterday in the street as we passed by his house. He offered us a cold beer. I drank it down with *puro gusto*, sheer delight, after a morning of work.

Don Santiago's house was a simple one, an example of most homes here: sticks and old boards clung together, wrapped up in cords and rusting, bent nails. He has no electricity, and just one faucet of running water.

I suppose when he saw us coming, he ran to the nearest store and bought the frosty beers. He wanted to thank us for the help that we gave his wife during the birth of their son. It was not very much, just a ride from the hospital. He grinned as I drank down the beer, almost as if getting a kick out of the fact that a gringo missioner would enjoy alcohol, guilt-free.

There was only one road from the nation's capital to Poptún, and on that road there existed only one busline, *La Fuente del Norte*, The Northern Source. Lately, however, it has earned the name *La Fuente de la Muerte* by our neighbors. The Source of Death.

Last night one of the buses flipped over, due to the fact that it was overfilled with two loads of people.

One vehicle down in the capital was not working. Instead of waiting, the owner decided to stuff this one full with both sets of passengers. Several sat on top of the vehicle, holding onto the tied baggage on the luggage rack. The driver tried to pull the bus over a steep incline just outside of Poptún, but didn't make it. The brakes failed. The bus rolled backwards and flipped over the cliff.

Several people were killed. Almost everyone on board was wounded, especially the ones inside. Those who could began walking to Poptún. An army truck picked up some of the wounded, but the dead had to be left behind, as nightfall was coming. The army was not one to stay out after dark, fearing guerrilla reprisals.

The whole town showed up at the health clinic, looking for relatives, dead or wounded. Most flocked about for curiosity's sake, wondering if any friends were inside. The clinic called the local Catholic Church, which had its own health program and a supply of medicines. We carried over some boxes of basic medical materials and glucose drips to the hospital. The clinic was accustomed to borrowing from the parish. They never have enough, to the point that they have to ask patients to go out and buy their own surgical equipment before coming in for an operation.

Outside the crowd counted the dead by the eruptions of tears in various corners of the multitude. "Padre Chamba will be busy in the cemetery this week," observed one man standing at my side.

Our home was a simple one, though more developed than most folks in the area. I painted the cement walls a light cream color to make it more cheerful, and I had the electrical work redone (only one light bulb dangled from the middle of the ceiling when we moved in). I also had a ceiling put into the kitchen area, as there was no ceiling before, just a big gap from wall to roof where the bats and mosquitoes flew.

Wooden walls that look like horse stables divided the large room into smaller quarters. The walls stopped two feet short of reaching the ceiling, so you heard everything and everybody else in the house. Privacy was limited to the latrine outside, where you were bothered only by doña Marina, the elderly woman who lived next door.

We had our own set of neighbors. Polo lived across the street with his wife Lidia. Polo was the young carpenter who put in my ceiling. In the far corner stood the store of doña Telma, the evangelist who named her establishment *El Renacimiento*

(The Rebirth). We bought our cokes and chips over there, but no beer. Right next to us was doña Selia, a woman in her thirties who acted as anchorwoman and investigative reporter for the neighborhood news. We enjoyed the experience of her talents. Our first week there she knocked on our door. Michelle answered. "Hello! I live next to you all. Listen, I think my macaw flew over the fence into your backyard. Mind if I check?"

Michelle showed her the way to the backdoor. Doña Selia's neck turned into rubber as she passed through the house. Her head moved from side to side to inventory how gringos live. She finally reached the back, where I stood working near the open door, cleaning up the yard. We chatted. She was very enthused about having new neighbors. Then I asked if she wanted to come on back and check on her macaw.

"Macaw? What ma . . . oh, YES! Yes, I believe it flew back into my yard, yes. I'm sure of it, but thank you . . . !"

On the other side of our house lived little doña Marina. She was quite old, and according to other neighbors, a little on the crazy side. "Gringa! Gringa!" she yelled while crossing over from her yard to ours, looking for Michelle. Though she could not find la gringa, Marina always knew where to find me. She approached the outhouse and peered over the top edges of the wood wall. She stared down at me like a wrinkled Kilroy.

"Where is the gringa?"

"I suppose she's in the house, doña Marina."

"Oh. What are you reading?"

"The newspaper, doña Marina."

"Oh. Well, I've got some grapefruits to give her. I hate grapefruits myself, but she seems to love them, I don't know why. . . ."

She walked off. I remained in fetus position, crunching the newspaper between my face and crotch. My body relaxed only when she walked a safe distance away.

I believe doña Marina was a *curandera,* or medicine woman. Perhaps she did not practice anymore, except on her new neighbors whenever they were standing out next to the compost pile. "How is your señora, the gringa? Is she sick? If she is, it's probably because she's stopped up. The best thing for that is a cricket. Take a cricket, and snap its two hind legs off here and here." She took a stick and pretended to cut her leg off at the pelvis and the knee. "Take those pieces and boil them in water until they crack open. Then take the tea and drink it with a little sugar, because it's bitter. You will pee all night, I tell you. You'll soak the bed. But it's worth it. It'll unstop you. I swear."

After a second bus accident from La Fuente, a rumor began among neighbors: The owner of the busline had made a pact with the Devil.

To verify this, I spoke with a number of people who did not necessarily know one another. They all told me the same story. Such a voice ran through the streets, in the market, in the stores, the churches: The owner was happy over bus accidents, as they fulfilled his part of the contract, handing over souls to the Devil. In turn, his income rose.

It was no surprise that his business proved financially successful. His was the only busline into the Petén jungle. Local people who needed to go south to visit family or spend time in the capital's hospitals had no choice but to board a bus. The high possibility of death became just one more factor in the people's planning of long trips.

People spoke of the pact every day. I could not disagree with them, knowing that a man *does* make a pact with the Devil whenever he chooses money over people's lives.

Two missioners from a church I had not heard of showed up at our house, and after several minutes of friendly chatter, one of the youths began to sell me their theology. The one who spoke was from Texas. He was a large, stout young man of twenty years. He spoke Spanish very fluently, though it was laced with an accent with deep roots in the white, U. S. South.

Both young men had blond hair and blue-eyes. The sun had burned their smiling cheeks. Michelle and I listened for a good long while (thus, I suppose, is courtesy, or stupidity), up until the moment that he said, "and the dark-skinned people, since they are the cursed of God. . . ."

I stopped his sermon. My dark-skinned lineage rose up in me. My mother, whose photo hung on the wall just behind the Texan, had obvious indigenous roots. I told him that I was not only surprised but extremely angry hearing such discriminatory language, and that we were not going to hear in our home any more of such racism and white supremacy, wrapped up in a cloak of gospel passages.

The young man began to weep. So brainwashed was he that he did not realize what he was saying. His companion hid himself around the corner of the kitchen. The large Texan who had stood preaching now sat down on the floor, crying, asking for forgiveness, saying that in no way did he mean to sound racist. They left quickly, two Aryan puppies with their tails hiding between kicked-up legs.

While standing before the two preachers in my kitchen, my mother's blood rose up in me. I remembered once when an old girlfriend called me on the phone years ago and affectionately greeted me, "Hello, Spic," and I said nothing. My mother heard her say it as she hung up on the other line.

Later Mom asked, in a voice of anger and tears, "Don't you have any respect for your heritage? Aren't you proud to be Latino?" She spoke from years of discrimination, from the days that people called her "Apache" and "light-skinned nigger" while she walked down small town streets in East Tennessee.

Because of her, I know that I am Latino. I grow more cognizant of this when my mother's blood boils up and lashes out to sting back the new puppies of racism, such as the young missioners.

They never came back to visit.

Pacifying the little devils: According to our neighbor doña Selia, another accident of the Northern Source happened in Puerto Barrios, about five hours south of here: "From what I understand," explained Selia, "the contract between the owner and the Devil demands the loss of six buses. Somehow through these accidents the owner will make more money. But if he doesn't fulfill his part, he will lose his life, as well as his children. So the owner is sending out the worst buses of his fleet, always filling them up with two loads of people. Can you believe that?"

A number of us stood about, buying colas from doña Telma's evangelical store, listening to Selia's freshest news. Not one of us doubted her.

OF KIDNAPPINGS
AND OTHER LOSSES

I had never heard of the name Dianna Ortiz before. Yet in the next few weeks that name would be on every missioner's lips. In the months that followed, Ortiz would be mentioned by both guerrilla soldiers and army officials. Later, after it was all over, she would be interviewed by the likes of Diane Sawyer on a U.S. television news show.

Yet on the day that Michelle and I drove into Guatemala City for a pregnancy checkup, Dianna Ortiz was but another nun-missioner among a scattering of missioners across the country of Guatemala.

We had walked into the Maryknoll Missioner residence in the city, tired from the long trip but happy over the possible news that Michelle was showing signs of pregnancy. We met a friend there named Lisa. It was a pleasant surprise to see her, until we found out why she too visited the city house. "A friend of mind has been kidnapped," she told us.

Lisa had been with Dianna at a retreat in Antigua, a small colonial tourist town just down the road. As they all took a break for the day, Dianna had wandered into the back garden of the convent to pray. Unknown men had entered through an opening in the wall, had abducted Dianna, and had then disappeared with her.

Lisa and others returned to the missioner residence in the city in order to begin searching. They made contact with every group they had access to, from U.S. newspapers to Amnesty International. Some of us stayed close to the phones in order to wait for a signal, either a ransom note or a call about new data, whether or not Dianna had been found, or whether or not she was alive. To watch our friend Lisa, a woman in her early thirties, was to see the face of that fear that reacts to something worse than death: disappearance. Yet the fear did not paralyze her. Lisa kept moving, rousing up everyone she could to get involved in the finding of her friend.

Michelle and I stood in a strange place. She had an appointment to make concerning her possible pregnancy. With little for us to be able to do, we made the appointment. The doctor gladly told us the good news, that yes, she was expecting.

That night there was still no word on Dianna Ortiz. The Archbishop of Central America had been called. He, too, placed his powerful word toward the finding of the missing nun. Her name came across national television and radio. Before the night was over, international human rights groups made sure the rest of the world knew as well.

The phone rang throughout the next day. Newspapers, television stations, and policemen wanted to know why the Maryknoll house had stuck its nose in the incident. Army officials demanded to know what information the house had on the whereabouts of the young woman. In the frenzy of the day, with people running through the house to send faxes and make connections that put pressure on certain powers that control death squads, the phone rang. It was Dianna.

They met her at a travel agency that most missioners had used to make international flight arrangements. She had hidden there after escaping from her abductors. They drove her back to our mission house, hiding her in the backseat so that the police outside would not know that the entering car carried the now-famous victim. Lisa walked her quickly into the house and up the stairs. The two women turned the corner, where Michelle and I stood. Dianna Ortiz looked at us but did not see us. Her hands and arms bundled over her chest, as if to hide the scars upon her face and neck. On the side of her neck I noticed round black marks that later I would learn were a line of cigarette burns. I held Michelle's hand at that moment, and felt her body shudder. As Dianna stared at us as if we were individuals of the fellow dead, Lisa rushed her by.

"Can we use your room? We've got to take pictures of her wounds. Your room has better lighting."

We obliged and watched as they disappeared behind the closed door.

The tension did not end. It only changed its shape, mutating itself from the frenzy of the search inside the house, to the presence of the police and army spies on the street.

Government entities placed a continuous surveillance upon us. The U.S. Embassy also demanded to know what was going on, as they promised to offer the best of security. Yet such a thought shot fear through Dianna. We would soon learn that, while abducted, Dianna recognized a gringo voice among the Spanish speaking torturers, one who said something about having a friend at the Embassy.

A priest named Dan, a fellow who has lived most of his fifty-odd years in Central America, walked into the house. Dan was of a teddy bear stature, with a large walrus moustache. "What's with all the cops outside?" he asked. Someone filled him in. Dan sat and visited awhile, then walked to the kitchen. He came back out with a large plate of doughnuts and cups of coffee. Then he walked out the door.

Lisa sat in a rocking chair, weary from the day. Yet Dan made her curious. "Hey, what are you going to do with that?"

"Take it out to our friends outside."

"What?" asked Lisa, incredulous.

"They're cops, aren't they? This is the international peace sign for all police forces." He smiled and lifted up the snack.

Twenty minutes later he walked back in with an empty plate. "I just stood next to their squad car while they ate. They were very nice. I asked them why they were out here. They told me that they were here to watch us. I asked why. They said they didn't know."

The missioners who gathered in the living room drank sodas and beer and tried to rest from the crisis. They talked, and even found some levity in the moment so as to remind themselves of some remnants of normal life. Michelle and I visited for awhile. Then we excused ourselves for the evening and went upstairs to our room, where we watched and whispered over the blood that slipped out of Michelle's womb. We had seen the signs of miscarriage before, and knew that this was no different. We gathered together as a couple must, and we sat in the silence of a house that waited for the heavy wave of sequestered anxiety to wash away, while police officers and army spies walked upon the sidewalks outside, glancing toward us from time to time.

Though the police stood outside, Dianna was already gone. The Papal Nuncio himself, the cleric who is the Pope's representative in each country, arrived at the missioner house and offered his body and life as protection. It was perhaps the highest form of security Dianna could receive. In a country that suffers from a systematic oppression that creates every entity from dire poverty to death squads, the spiritual vicars of the Roman Catholic Church still have that certain power to make fellow Latinos bow and humble themselves.

The U.S. Embassy protested, declaring that this was a job that they must fulfill. Yet the vicar quietly showed up in his private limousine. Dianna was driven to the international airport. The vicar walked her all the way to the plane, got her to her seat, blessed her, and walked off. He stood at the door of the jet until the flight attendant closed it. He did not leave the airport until he saw the plane disappear behind low clouds.

Later the details of the abduction came to light. Yet it was still difficult to make sense of the story. Dianna was not involved in any political or subversive work that would have provoked such actions by governmental forces. She taught children in a parochial school. It was said that a photo was taken of her when she first came into the country. In the photo she is ostensibly standing in a crowd of people in the middle of Guatemala City as they watched a march go by, one promoted by GAM ("Grupo de Apoyo Mutuo," a support group that had lost family members to the systematic violence). From that point on she received written death threats. Men had approached her in public places and had whispered fear into her ear. She, not understanding the seriousness of the situation, continued to work in the school.

They took her as she prayed in the backyard of the Antigua convent. They made her board a bus and told her to say nothing lest they open up a grenade and kill all the people on board. Then they got in a police car that took them to a warehouse outside of the small town. In the warehouse, a distance away from any ears, they began their work.

When Lisa took pictures of Dianna in our bedroom, she counted 111 cigarette burns all over the woman's body. It was plain to see that she had been raped a number of times in the hours that she was missing. The other signs could not be seen so readily. When Dianna began to work through the images of that twenty-four hour period, she could see the men who threw her into a pit filled with cadavers, where they left her for hours at a time. She could see the faces who hovered over her as she was beaten. One abductor said to a man in another room, "Hey Alejandro, come over here and have some fun." The man named Alejandro did enter. He cursed in English, then spoke in Spanish with the lilt of a gringo. "Idiots! She is a North American. Let her alone! It's all over the fucking newspapers! The *International* news is talking about her!"

Alejandro gave her back her clothes and drove her away from the warehouse that echoed with others' groans. She sat in the passenger seat while he calmly explained to her that this was all a mistake. "You see, we were looking for someone else, and they mistook you for that person. There's no real need to take this wrong, it was just an error on our part. I can get you to a friend of mind at the U.S. Embassy now."

Dianna did not wait around to hear any more. At a red light in the center of Guatemala City she opened the door and dashed into the crowd of shoppers on the sidewalk. She made her way through familiar streets toward the travel agency. Dianna was of Mexican descent, and her skin color acted as a camouflaged blessing that hid her away from the eyes of the gringo.

Dianna's abduction put Guatemala back in the international news once again. We watched CNN and ABC Nightly News, waiting to see when during the holy half-hour of world news Sister Ortiz would make it to the headlines. Yet she was still but a blip created by the information spin doctors in the United States.

Within the country the Guatemalan government and

army made it clear that they were the true victims of a crazed, savaged lesbian who kidnapped herself and who made up the whole story to protect her relationship with a sadistic lover.

We made our way back to Poptún. Michelle walked carefully through life, trying to block out all incidents around her so as to protect that which bled inside her. A necessary sense of survival came over her as she lay in bed. The doctor had warned her to move very little, to stay in bed for at least three weeks so as to do everything in her grasp to save the pregnancy. She followed orders. Friends came by and visited. They prayed over her and gave her advice on how to take care of herself, everything from putting her feet upon the wall to eating duck eggs. Yet the life continued to slip out of her as if unable to survive certain waves of anxieties, ones that human beings should live without.

We buried the tiny fetus in the backyard of our home. We said a quiet prayer over the grave, then quickly returned to our lives. Among friends we spoke of how a nun's abduction created reverberations throughout the country. As a couple we moved on from our own private loss and pretended that life cannot stop.

Thousands of miles away a woman named Dianna Ortiz, who knew nothing of us, began a long prayer over the grave of her own life. In Chicago she joined with a group of other victims of torture who worked collectively to move through the grave that they had been forced to wander in. To live became her radical act.

CHAPTER FOUR

THE CHILD WHO
ROSE FROM THE DEAD

I awoke to a scream that raised the sheets off the bed. It was 1:00 a.m., I saw by the small watch on the endtable, and that high-pitched yelp would not end. I forgot where I was or why a wail pierced the whole room, until Michelle reminded me, "It's your turn."

Then I remembered that nameless one who had been sleeping in our bedroom.

The diaper needed changing. Forty-eight hours previous I could not even approach him whenever it was time to do this. Now I dexterously unwrapped him, lifted his legs, cleaned, wiped, and ducked my head so he didn't pee on me. After some Desitin cream smeared on the butt, I rewrapped him with a clean diaper. He looked up with large, walnut eyes. The tears passed. He stretched his whole dark-skinned body and yawned as if to say, "There. You know, that's all I really wanted."

After feeding him a bottle, I returned to bed. My heart

no longer pounded. The bottle seemed to have calmed me as much as it did him.

He had no name, no documents or papers. He was most assuredly a Kekchi, you could see that in his hair and coffee-colored skin. Poor, of course. He was two months old and weighed seven pounds. His arms dangled from his shoulders like lean pieces of wood that splintered into fingers at the ends. He was, however, adorable, especially when he looked straight at you.

Hunger had eaten away at his mother's mind. She would never remember leaving him in the woods on the outskirts of town. There he had remained for three days. Another woman heard his screams and found him. She could barely distinguish between his clothes and the mud, rainwater, and feces. Ants crawled over him.

No one could find the mother. The father, who worked in fields far from Poptún, knew nothing of the incident. The woman brought the child to the local judge. A policeman's wife took care of him for five days. Then he came to our home.

It was interesting to see who agreed and disagreed with this decision. A few fellow missioners from the States thought it unwise. "You just recently had a miscarriage," said one woman named Sheila. "Do you think this is a good idea?" Yet a couple of neighbors smiled in delight as they came by to visit the baby who had been found in the woods. "God sent him your way," said Oli, a friend from around the corner.

I could not determine who sent the boy here. I could, however, see the change in my wife. Michelle fed him and changed him with a coo of perfect patience. I remained quiet to any cavils as I watched her enjoy a transient moment of motherhood.

For three more days our lives circled around the boy. We took him to the health center for a checkup. We bought bottles and diapers. Neighbors chipped in and collected a large pile of clothes. When we walked the streets, children and mothers gathered around us, googly-eyed over the little one. Everyone knew who he was, *el abandonado*, the abandoned one.

The father had taken his wife to the capital to place her in a hospital for the mentally disabled. He planned to return to Poptún the following Monday. I asked his brother, "What is the father's name?"

"Lázaro," said the sibling.

"Well, for now, we'll just call this one Lazarito. I don't like calling him 'the kid,' or the 'baby.'"

Yet I continued to call him "baby." In refusing to place a name upon him, I lied to myself, and believed the lie.

I asked when Lázaro would return. The brother reassured me, on Monday. "*Lo quiere muchísimo*," he said. "The Dad loves the boy so much." He explained that this was Lázaro's only child. Of course, of course, and Michelle and I breathed out relief, knowing that the father indeed loved this child. We knew that the boy would go back home to a family that wanted him.

Everyone in our neighborhood thought differently. They used the word *regalar* often in conversation, to give as a gift. "Perhaps the father will give him to you all. They are so poor, they would probably want the best for him, and thus would want you all to have him."

We chuckled at that, saying no, no, that would not do, because Lázaro, "Lo quiere muchísimo," and we could not take his son who he loves so very much. Yet the idea planted deeply into our hearts. To *gift* a child for the sake of the child could be a venerable act. To accept such a gift would be so very easy.

Yet as Monday approached us, the panic of doubt pooled in the recesses of our thoughts. Michelle spoke as a mother, arguing with me over the well-being of the child. I fought with a logic that was not my own. She shut down, then handed me the boy whose eyes encircled the room. "Here, take Lazarito," she mumbled, and fled to the back of the house.

Monday came, but the father did not. All day we waited for him. The hours turned against us. The little one kept us busy, but each time we changed a diaper and fed him and burped him, a ghostly umbilical cord snapped around us like a fetus taken too quickly from the womb. Sheila offered us her truck so we could find Lázaro's village and deliver the baby.

They lived outside of San Luís, about an hour away. We drove to the local parish rectory. A woman named Delia who worked for the church offered to take us to the edge of town. Michelle said her goodbye to the little one, kissing him on the forehead. She turned away as I walked out the door. I heard my wife wail for the first time in our married life, a woman whose motherhood had been taken from her twice in one season.

A priest named Joe walked with me. We followed Delia to the outskirts of San Luís, through rolling hills and on pathways that took us away from the center of town. We could no longer hear the rattle of trucks that passed over the town's dirt street. This was the *campo*, the countryside. Joe carried two bags filled with diapers, formula, medicine, clothes, baby bottles. I carried the sleeping boy. I wondered if he sensed the return to familiar surroundings.

We arrived at the small, dilapidated *champa,* a building made of thin, round sticks tied together. We stared through the cracks at the dirt floor protected by a straw roof. This was not new to me. I protected my heart by saying so, not new to me at all, I have seen poverty before, this does not affect me.

The father was not home. He was held up in the fields, tending to his responsibilities regarding survival. We looked for his mother-in-law's home. I held tight to the boy to protect him from a muddy fall. After about twenty minutes of walking through these hills of banana trees and mud paths, we found it. A neighbor woman, obviously Kekchi by her indigenous, colorful dress, lead the way. All eyes fell upon us. This house was the same: one room, small, poor. I had seen all of this before. They all gathered around, children, mothers, a couple of men. They stared at the gringo who held one of their own. They all knew the story about the mother who had left him in the woods. It was no small miracle in their eyes that he had returned alive.

They offered me a seat. Many of them only spoke Kekchi, so the neighbor woman translated for me as I explained in Spanish the medicines and his sickness. "He has thrush on his tongue, these drops are for that, and he is very malnourished, so here are some vitamins." We talked about feeding him. One woman there told me that a relative of the boy was also breast-feeding a child, and she could breast-feed him too. My heart leapt at that. I knew that breast milk could save his life, and in that moment his life held me in the grip of a baby palm.

We chatted for a short while, warming ourselves in our new acquaintance. Soon it was time to go. The one woman holding the boy smiled at me as I muttered, "Well, I better say goodbye." Then too much tumbled out of my mouth, "Yes, he was with us for four days. But it was no bother at all. You see, we have no children, and my wife, she was more than happy to take care of him, it brought her a great deal of joy—." I stopped myself, and added, "But I can see, he is very happy here, with his family." I faked a smile.

One of the women said to me from behind, oh yes, it is good to see him, for you see, Lázaro the father, "Lo quiere muschísimo."

This resounded too deeply. No chance of regalar. Today was not the day for gift-giving. Nor should it be. Regalar is a radical act of mutual consent. Now was only for saying goodbye. I bent down and kissed him on the forehead. "Goodbye, Lazarito," said I, using my name for him for the first time.

He looked up at me with walnut eyes one final time. I saw that he was back where he was born. He was not in our home, which, in all its simplicity, was a lifetime away from this shack and this poverty. I looked around me and saw the poor as they all smiled upon me in appreciation. I saw their community, a network of people who took care of their own. They became one body before me, an entity that utilized simple homes as mere survival from the elements, and who relied on a collective strength to endure. As they turned to the babe to care for him, "It does not affect me" was no longer true. The air itself overwhelmed me. I walked away quickly, passing Father Joe, and held closed lungs filled with a new sadness that stripped the umbilical cord from me.

Joe caught up with me and gave gringo advice that actually fell through me like a rush of fresh water. "That was a hell of a thing to do, taking care of that boy," he muttered.

"Don't ever do it again." He chuckled good-naturedly and slapped me on the back.

Perhaps I would take heed to his advice. To not do it again meant to not feel this specific pain. All this could have been avoided four days previous with a quick, "No, I'm sorry, we can't take a child in right now." Ours was no act of charity. We desired with a longing that blinds a person from risk. Perhaps such a desire is the trap of a human condition that propels us deeper into hope, yet not without severe cuts from the plunge.

We returned to a silent house. Michelle and I shared some whiskey before going to bed. We awoke to old schedules, cleaning up the house, making coffee, preparing for the day. We followed known patterns, without him screaming at us for attention, without the responsibility, the dirty diapers, the boiling of milk bottles. We returned to our places; to emptiness, filled for a transient moment. I wrote these words in the tranquility of a young man who has all the time in the world. Yet the longing had been planted. The child who rose from the dead was also the one who stood before our living tomb and screamed at us to awaken.

CHAPTER FIVE

VIGNETTES

Michelle and I run along the *pista*, the two-mile long dirt and gravel airstrip that stretches alongside Poptún. Built by the army long ago, it is now rarely used. Low noises emanate from the small hills surrounding us. The animals follow behind. Slowly their large heads roll upward to be seen over a hill. The five tanks move over the earth like gigantic turtles growling forward, grumbling people out of their way. They cross the dirt road, drive behind the very modern control tower, then pull up in front of doña Anita's adobe house and park in her front yard. Doña Anita cannot see the tanks from her window, for she is dying of uterine cancer in her bed. But her son Carlos can, and he carefully puts his head to the side of the door and watches. We all watch, wondering where they have been, what they have done.

Individuals follow their daily routines around the pista. Indigenous Kekchi women and men carry machetes in one hand and a load of firewood or babies on their backs. All bend their heads towards the growling machines that have decided to park for lunch on dying doña Anita's front field. All watch with a pensive curiosity. Michelle and I keep running, all the way home.

We walk home after a church meeting, excited about the success of the gathering. We turn the corner to our home just as a blast of dust rolls over us. Through the cloudy grit we see a large green army truck that did the trick, full to the brim with *Kaibiles*.

Kaibiles are the military special forces in Guatemala, also known as the Angels of Death. Their motto: We are killing machines.

All of them are young. Many of them are indigenous and have been forced into the service. They stare out at the town the truck has just entered, with their purple berets cocked to one side, their bodies strong and sinewy and ready for any encounter. We look over toward the pista at the regular foot soldiers standing by with M-16s in their hands. They protect the empty airstrip. A few seconds later the whip of two huge propellers falls, then roars itself into reverse as an army personnel plane lands on the airstrip.

Civilians stand to the side, waiting for permission to cross the runway in order to go home. Michelle and I rush into the house to escape the billows of dust.

The electricity has been on for half-days the past two weeks. From six at night to six in the morning we have lights. We spend part of the days trying to guard food in the refrigerator, barely opening its door so as not to let the cold escape. After six o'clock we read and listen to the radio, enjoying the concept of electricity until bedtime. Rumor has it the guerrillas blew up five tank trucks of diesel that are used to fuel the local electric plant. Now no truck driver wants to drive into the Petén, afraid of an encounter with the G-forces. The state of the Petén is virtually cut off. The towns rely entirely on outside resources, and the only road into this state now has little business traffic. This perhaps explains the heavy movement of the army.

In Poptún, we never see the war. Our town is more of a training ground for the soldiers. In these days more trucks of soldiers leave town, supposedly to protect Poptún from the guerrillas. The Guatemalan army, however, is famous for not confronting the guerrillas, but for burning down whole villages and slaughtering groups of people at a time.* Meanwhile, we complain about our refrigerator and how rough life is without electricity.

A friend named Cristina who lives down the street about two blocks hardly gives any of this a thought. She has never had the luxury of electricity. She has always lit candles at

*Military strategies designed and implemented by the Guatemalan Army have been well documented in the past few years. According to The Guatemalan Church in Exile, the army carried out scorched-earth campaigns throughout various regions of the country, killing off large numbers of the rural population by decapitation and burning down homes with families trapped inside. For more information, see *Guatemala, Security, Development, and Democracy* published by The Guatemalan Church in Exile, 1989. Pp. 69–70.

night in order to cook and to clean. She has never guarded food in an icebox, but rather partakes in daily obtained bread. In bed, exhausted after a long day of work, doña Cristina blows out the candle, thinking little of guerrillas or refrigerators.

I tell a story to a group of children, about a hunting dog named Blue who ran so fast into a tree that he split himself in two. When I put him back together again, he lived, but I slapped him back together sloppily, so now he has two feet up and two feet down. They listen with their eyes as well as their ears. They don't say a word, as they are deep into the images. Children remind me that belief makes nothing real, while story creates reality. Behind us, their mother Julia laughs into the wash basin while she scrubs clothes clean.

Children also gather around the front of our house while I play guitar. One girl named Patricia works on some embroidery. Michelle brings out her own needlepoint, and soon the girls *and* boys have left the guitarist with empty space before him. They crowd around Michelle's work. Two mothers come by, and everyone excitedly exchanges ideas and how-to's on other embroidery pieces. I play *Blackbird* upon the strings, offering background music.

We attend Kekchi mass in a village about six miles out of town. Father Chamba is Q'achiq'el, another branch off the Maya root. For him the Maya customs are the first true

religion of Guatemala, and he happily participates in the blessing of this new little church out in the mountains. He follows
behind the four *mayordomos*, the elders of a community, who
are the leaders elected by their people. One of their responsibilities is the upkeep of their customs, especially in relationship
with the local Catholic church. The old men light candles in four
corners of the new building. Our mayordomo, a woman, flings
a can of burning, fuming incense from one side to the next,
filling the room with smoke that lifts our prayers through the
windows and out to the god of the earth, god of corn, god of life
and shadows, god of death and food. Afterward the Catholic
mass begins.

In his sermon Father Chamba speaks of rights given by
God. "In God's plan, there are no government and reforms that
steal the earth we live on. There are no corrupt government
plans that take the land from poor farmers who have worked the
earth for two thousand years. There is no institution that hands
over all the farmland to the rich landowners. There is justice in
God's heaven, there is truth in God's plan."

I watch and listen from a pew. His are words that, in the
eyes of those rich landowners and the military, are illegal. They
are statements worthy of a death squad penalty. Padre Chamba
is thirty-two years old. He lost both his parents and an aunt to
death squads. A band of soldiers raped his sister, chaining her
down to a truck bed while they violated her.

Padre Chamba is what we call *decidido*, resolute, deter-
mined. History has made him that way. He is one man I can say
who has faith, who is truly not afraid.

I watch this good man who is becoming a friend. I listen

to what he says. I pick at every sentence and phrase to see what is safe to say and what is a necessary risk.

The helicopter flies over our house as if it wants to slice the tin roof off. It lands on the edge of town at the *comandancia*, the training ground for the Kaibiles. Gringo soldiers walk down. They are mostly blond and blue-eyed, easy to pick out in a crowd. They have come to train these Kaibiles to be even better at their work.

The U.S. soldiers remain in town for two weeks. We see them running around in a Toyota van, buying up furniture from our neighbor Polo who is a carpenter (end tables made of pure mahogany, a common wood here). The soldiers dine in tiny restaurants after a full day of teaching Rambo tactics to Guatemalan special forces.

Strange, but I vaguely remember some international law that prohibits the training of military personnel who serve a country with a dubious human rights record.

The military gringos are everywhere. They play their war games in the training camp and helicopters. Bombs and rockets fire off from time to time during their stay. Their paratroopers fall from the choppers, mixed in among the dozens of Kaibiles. They all float down, and the whole town stretches its neck up in silent curiosity.

Mass always begins at ten o'clock in Poptún. Well, okay, ten after ten (we *are* in Latin America, you know). Michelle and

I get a seat next to Mila, a young woman who gave birth to a boy just a few months ago. Michelle attended her labor. The two have become close over the months.

During the Our Father, a dog runs between our legs. This is common; dogs have been known to passively participate in church here, falling asleep beside their masters in the aisle. I have never heard a bark in mass.

By the middle of the prayer another dog passes through and knocks against Michelle's shin bone. It is obviously confused in this forest of legs. By the time of the sign of peace, two other dogs have come through. It seems the first dog is in heat. This could get ugly.

Mila, Michelle, and others around us all exchange the sign of peace, then quickly stand on top of the kneelers and try to ignore the love affair below us.

Old doña Marina approaches me with an armful of grapefruits. "These are for the gringa. I hear she likes them. I don't understand why. Bitter as hell."

We speak for several minutes. Actually I listen as the old curandera tells me of her recent aches and pains. She asks a question that breaks the monotone of her cavils. "Is it true that your gringa lost a baby?"

Surprised, I respond affirmatively.

"Yes. It was during that time when the gringa nun was kidnapped in the city. You were there, that's what Michelle told me. Said that she shuddered all over when she saw that poor sister." It is the first time I have heard doña Marina use my wife's name. "You saw that nun. She saw you and Michelle. Those who tortured her, they killed your baby. They hurt the nun with the *mal ojo*, and when she looked at you, those bastards who hurt her also hurt Michelle. The evil eye is strong. It penetrates good people with its badness."

I can hear little more. I back away from the elderly woman with the grapefruits now in my arm. I rush my goodbyes and move to my back door.

I walk by the bus depot. Among the small crowd of indigenous people sits the young Texan missioner who I had kicked out of my house weeks previous. His face has never become accustomed to the intense jungle heat. Red splotches stain his cheeks and neck. He lowers his glasses to clean sweat off the lenses.

I approach him, hoping our heated discussion over his racist theologies could be put to the side a moment. Once he sees me he sits back slightly, as if braced for any dirt that I plan to kick in his face.

We exchange salutations. "What's going on?" I ask.

"I'm heading home. To Texas."

"Oh. Is your time up here?"

"No. But I just can't get through to these people." He looks up and down the street at the townsfolk who pass by. "I mean, they just don't respond. I did a variety show the other night at my church. A lot of people showed up. I did some of my best standup comedy, stuff that I used back in college. It was really funny back then. But here, nobody laughed. I felt like a dufus up there."

We talk a few minutes more. "Good luck in Texas," I say.

"Yeah, thanks. Lord knows I tried here." He looks up the road as if to rush the bus his way. "But this place is truly what is meant by God-forsaken. Just no God at all in these people."

"Don Marcos! Doña Michelle! Is Chelena in here? We can't find her!"

It is nine o'clock at night. The girls peer into our kitchen, asking for the three-year-old daughter of a neighbor. Michelle grabs a flashlight. We walk outside into the obscurity of the street in front of our house. Thoughts run into your mind, some of them common in any country, others that are particular to this one: She has wandered off into another neighborhood; somebody in a truck picked her up and carried her out of town; she has wandered onto the runway. (Are their soldiers out there now? Are there Kaibiles?)

Michelle beams the light into the moonless night. On the other side of the street we see the women who have been searching, now all gathered into doña Telma's corner store. Michelle shines her light onto little Deborah's face, another neighborhood kid. "We found her!" she yells. "She was asleep under her mother's bed. . . ."

She had fallen asleep on the floor, and in one stretch and a yawn had rolled a couple of times, right under the bedframe. She is still sleeping there. Her mother and sister and all the neighborhood women gather in doña Telma's corner store to laugh about the incident. They watch some television on the little black-and-white screen that sits on the shelf between fresh eggs and bananas. Michelle chats with doña Marina. The elderly curandera offers Michelle another natural cure for some ailment, though Michelle is not the least bit sick. I try to ignore the old woman. I magically pull a coin out of one little girl's ear, leaving her to pick at her head for more.

Soon we say goodnight. We prepare for bed. We pull down the mosquito net and curl up under the sheets. These have been long days. Some have been difficult. We fall asleep. The dreams come, mixing desire and memory, putting together this country and ours. Doña Telma offers colas to my mother. The house of Michelle's parents stands here in Poptún, just down the street from ours. I amble through dreams, walking between two realities, longing for both.

CHAPTER SIX

GUNSHOTS, AMOEBAS, AND OTHER INCIDENTALS

Yesterday we walked to a barrio named Santa Fe to visit the house of don Chepe and doña Evangelina. We sat down in the kitchen made of cracked wood and a thatched roof with a dirt floor cluttered with old, rotted chairs. We chatted about life around town, about the church, then about his kids. "We had five, but one of them died."

"Oh, I'm sorry. What did he die of? Sickness?"

"No. no. He wasn't sick. It was an accident. We're still very sad over it, though it happened over a year ago."

Don Chepe began the account of what occurred one Saturday when he walked out to work in the cornfield. He took the two brothers Tomás and Mateo with him, so as to pass the day together. The neighborhood kids also went to play somewhere in the woods and fields, carrying with them their father's rifle as a toy. In one moment Tomás and Mateo ran into the other boys. They were all playing together. The gun went off. The bullet pierced Tomás' heart.

The owners of the rifle blamed don Chepe for not being on top of the situation, since he was the only adult nearby when the accident happened. Don Chepe was thrown in jail for two weeks. His oldest son, who works as a civilian for the army, paid the fine of 600 quetzales (about $110). Don Chepe stayed under surveillance for the following six months. He was not allowed to go out in the fields to work.

I asked who was the one who shot Tomás. Chepe said, "That boy over there," and he barely raised a weak finger to the other son named Mateo who stood in a corner's shadow.

The boy looked at me. I realized that he had been in that corner all during our visit without moving. He looked at Michelle and me with obscure eyes that trembled with the vision of the gunshot. The bullet that killed his brother had left a lesion in Mateo's sight. He stood motionless with his hands dangling to the sides of his waist like some timid spirit haunting the house.

His mother told him to prepare coffee for the visitors. He obeyed. He poured the water and mixed the coffee in an old, blackened pot. He had trouble opening the sugar jar. I took it and unscrewed it, then I handed it back to him, touching his arm with my fingers. He turned to me and stared through the gunshot wound toward a lost boyhood.

Boiling water has become a part of life for us. Every three to four days we fill a huge pot that covers three eyes of the gas stove. It has to reach a boil (which takes about an hour and a half), then it must boil for twenty minutes so as to kill any and all parasites, amoebas, and cysts.

All the missioners in the Petén boil their water. Many teach this method in the health formation classes at the center. Unfortunately for most people, boiling water becomes an economic issue: to clean the water means using up a great deal of firewood every other day, and wood is not cheap. The average campesino has to decide between firewood and beans; which is more important, to keep the kids from getting parasites, or making sure the kids eat that night?

We can boil our water all we want, but that doesn't mean we'll never get sick. Visiting folks, we're always offered something cold to drink. I've gotten pretty good at tossing the lemonade out the window while the hostess turns her back to flip tortillas on the stove. I have to deal with the guilt of such hypocrisy and basic bad manners. Yet I've been sick enough times with parasites that I'd prefer to break a cultural courtesy from time to time.

Then there are missioners who were blessed by the Almighty with lead-lined stomachs. Father Jim, for example, or Santiago by Spanish name. Originally from Oklahoma, he's been in Central America for thirty-five years. They say he has never suffered stomach ailments. I've visited a couple of villages with him. After celebrating mass he'll take a cup of cold coffee and drink it down like it's the richest potable ever offered him. A week later he's fine. Meanwhile I'm visiting the latrine every half-hour.

Last week Padre Santiago and Michelle went to a local barrio to celebrate mass. After services the crowd went to the home of don Sebastian, the mayordomo of the Kekchi community. It was a beautiful celebration in itself, the handing out of tamales, the sharing of cacao, both of which are sacred foods among the Maya descendants. Michelle was captured by the autochthony of the moment. She also cringed at watching some of the women who threw cupfuls of creek water into the chocolate. She and Padre Santiago, as representatives of the parish house and guests of the barrio, were served first. Michelle thought she could just put her drink to the side while everyone else imbibed. Unfortunately the protocol was to have everyone present drink from the same gourds of chocolate. Jim and Michelle were given the first gourds.

"Oh God," whispered Michelle, "I just know this one is going to get me."

"Now, now," reassured Jim, "All you gotta do is drink it down real quick, and all those little parasites and amoebas and any other little animal will just slip down your throat through your intestines and straight out of you later on." With that, he downed his gourd, smacked his lips, and handed it back with a smile to the hostess. "Gracias, Señora."

Yesterday we carried the cadaver of a five-year-old girl back to her family's village. The parasite-infested body lay in the Poptún clinic. We bought the coffin from Rolando, the carpenter, who was just hammering on the final piece when I arrived. A fellow Church worker named Francisco and I put the body in the box. She was still warm when we picked her up. After placing her in the box, Francisco and I hammered away.

"Please return the bedsheet to us," asked one of the

clinic employees as we walked out with the filled coffin, "because we don't have extras, we're always running out."

We promised to do so after delivering the body.

The eighteen-year-old mother, who had been with us all along, cried for the first time when she saw the coffin. She too suffered from malnourishment. We drove to the village. Michelle had the wheel as I sat in the back and leaned over the coffin that stuck out of the open jeep. The tires kicked up dust from behind and covered the coffin in layers, groping for the body in order to make it its own.

We drove into the village of Achotal. Francisco directed Michelle over the footpaths toward some houses in the center of the small community. The sun had just disappeared over distant hills. It left enough light for us to see one another, and for the community to see the coffin sticking out of our vehicle. Faces turned to one another and whispered in Kekchi the obvious. One man who stood next to the door of a house looked at us, then turned away, jerking his angry sight from the jeep. The mother struggled with the Nissan's door. She banged against it to make it let her out. Francisco reached over and pulled the handle. She ran out toward the man, her tremulous cries leaping ahead of her.

This is Francisco's village. He and I carried the fresh pine casket into the shack. He explained in their native language when the girl died. Whispers from old women flowed around the flickers of candles. We opened the casket, lifted the girl out, and pulled the bloody, stained sheet from her now cold body. I flung it into the back of the jeep.

We stumbled away from the mourning village. No one

showed us the door. Messengers of death, no matter how kind, are never welcome.

In Poptún it was our turn to prepare an altar in front of our house for the procession that was to pass through town that evening. It's a custom for people to put such altars out front so that the Holy Week procession may carry Jesus to their door during his walk to Calvary.

Michelle and I fixed ours up. The procession came. We sat outside and chatted with neighbors and watched as two hundred people stood before our door, praying Our Fathers and Hail Marys before our altar. Soon they left us to move on to other houses and other altars. We took ours down, chatted some more with doña Selia (the *Macaw lady*, as Chamba calls her), then went to bed.

I could not sleep. Insomnia gnawed at me, reminding me of the horrible bouts of sleeplessness I had gone through in Nicaragua. Once the chain begins to form, night after night, I find it difficult to break. I have passed nights staring at the ceiling until four in the morning, enough to drive one insane. Yet this insomnia was different. It had begun earlier in the day when I placed my fingers upon the body of the child cadaver.

For the second time in a week we went to the funeral of another child. Mauro, the son of Simona and Lorenzo, died of God knows what ailment. He was fifteen months old. Worms left his nose with the final breath. In the cemetery they wanted to open the box in order to say goodbye to him. As they cracked it open the family members leaned over and touched the babe. A communal wail of departure rose from the cemetery, *Goodbye Mauro, goodbye my sweet little son, pray for us, because you are with God, God will hear you . . . !*

Afterwards they covered him over once again, and I thought, such a raw, crude way of confronting reality. And healthier. It was better to look upon the face of the boy, whose half-opened eyes saw nothing, and whose opened mouth spilled forth the foamy remnants of the sickness.

Another burial of another child. Once again I was afraid of insomnia, but it did not curse me that night. Perhaps the sadness wearied me. We knew this boy's family well. Mauro's life and ours had touched in earlier days when he sat on Michelle's lap and stared at his mom while she served us coffee.

We buried him the evening of Mother's Day.

In the past couple of weeks we've visited the Finca Ixobel, that farm of gringo tourists that sets over to one side of town. Carol DeVine, the proprietress of a local restaurant called *La Fonda Ixobel*, is a nice, open person. When she saw us a few times coming in and out of her establishment, Carol realized that we were not other tourists, but that we lived here. "You should come over and have dinner with Mike and me," she invited us, "we always have lots of food."

She was not lying. They put out a spread for up to forty people a night. The place had no electricity, so they used a legion of candles. We sat in the kitchen with them and talked through the evening. Mike was from Iowa, so there was a natural connection with Michelle. He was much more quiet than Carol, perhaps more introverted; but once we sat down with him he had us rolling. "I went out horseback riding the day before we were going to spend Thanksgiving with Carol's parents in the States. The horse bucked and sent me flying. I fell right on my back and threw out every muscle from my shoulders to my butt. I crawled back from the field to the cabin, and when I pushed the door open with my face and slithered into the living room, Carol just put her hands on her waistline and looked down at me. 'You'll do anything to not spend Thanksgiving with my parents, won't you?'"

They have lived here for twenty years. They are no strangers to Poptún nor to Guatemala in general. Now, whenever we go shopping in the market, I hear their names mentioned in reference to buying produce such as eggs or chickens from his farm. It seems that they have gained a certain respect from the poptunecos. Mike is seen as a good *patrón*, a man who pays a little bit more to his workers.

We've eaten over at the finca a few times now. Last night, as we left their place, they walked us to our jeep. Mike handed me a couple of fruits, ones which I could not see in the moonless night. "They're called ayotes. Real sweet. I think you'll like them." True Guatemalan fashion, giving a little gift of fruit on your way out the door.

Michelle's artistic skills have proven to affect our work in a surprising way. Each Saturday morning several dozen people from all over the country come to the Church Hall to participate in an adult education class. Michelle and I facilitate the meetings.

In one of our first gatherings we realized how limited our "first world" upbringing was in preparing us for such experiences. Michelle and I are accustomed to using the written word in classes. The majority of people we work with in Poptún cannot read nor write. When I began leading the meetings, I asked a few individuals to help me with reading a piece from scripture or handing out leaflets with stories and lessons written on them. Though some could read, they were nervous standing before others and trying to read the words from the bible's pages. I could tell that I had, without meaning to, set them up for certain failure. These were men and women with whom I had shared meals, enjoyed long nights of discussions together, and who had gathered in church meetings to pray long, eloquent prayers that came from the very struggle of their day-to-day existence. The inability to read did not mean stupidity. Yet suddenly, with a bible in their hand, they were shut down into a shameful silence. I realized then that the printed matter in their hand, ostensibly sacred, was actually yet another oppressive two-by-four against their heads. Written words, which for me stood for grace and power and meaning, beat at my friends like silent battering rams.

So we had an idea: start a literacy class. There were such classes all over the country, initiated by church groups and government agencies. A number of people had taken advantage of them. For the time being, however, we needed other means of promoting adult education. Thus Michelle's drawing skills came to the fore.

One day she painted a picture of a common rural scene:

A man riding a horse through the woods. Behind him a woman walked, carrying a load of firewood on her shoulders. Behind her walked a little boy.

Although we had stumbled through our first session without any visual aids, now we had provoked a lively discussion of ideas and opinions with Michelle's drawing. "Oh, I know who that is," said one Kekchi woman named Wicha. Her arms were crossed over her chest. "That's my husband and me."

I looked over at Michelle. She picked up on the same acrid feel of the woman's words.

"Oh come now, Wicha," said a man named Pedro Lepe. "I've never seen you work that hard."

A few chuckled. Wicha did not. She still had her arms crossed.

"You know I work as hard as any woman," she said. "But look at that man. Sitting high on the animal, with that poor girl bent under the wood. Neither one of those men (referring to the boy) are helping her."

This led quickly to a discussion of women's and men's roles in the family. It took little time for the conversation to get heated. Not surprisingly, the men spoke more voraciously, defending some position that I think I could understand from my gut, but for some reason didn't have the nerve to defend. There were other women, however, who broke gender expectations and spoke their mind alongside Wicha.

"Who eats the most in the mornings?" said a younger woman named Clara. "The men. They gobble down the tortillas and beans and leave half the amount for the wife and kids."

"Yeah, but the man needs that food," said Pedro. "We're out in the fields all day. If we don't eat enough, we can't make it.

Look at this," he pointed toward his own ribs. "Do I look like a gringo?" He glanced toward me with an "excuse the necessary insult" look. "No. I'm as skinny as the next campesino. I need that food to work."

"But a woman needs it to get through her day too," retorted Clara. "Especially when she's pregnant. How many young expecting women end up in the hospital with low blood?"

This discussion lasted the entire morning. Michelle and I played small parts in it. The arguments continued after the meeting, when people walked slowly back to their barrios.

"I don't know if that was a good thing or bad," said Michelle. "We may have caused fights in every neighborhood in town."

Whether this was true or not, more people showed up the next week. If Michelle had been feeling bad about the previous Saturday's arguments, it wasn't apparent in her choice for this week's piece of art: A man taking his weekly hard-earned cash in one frame, spending it in a bar in another, showing up at home drunk in the third.

Wicha sat in the front of the group. Again she had her arms crossed. She glanced about the room, shaking her head affirmatively with an "Isn't *that* the truth?" look about her.

The discussion lasted through lunch. People went home. When we visited folks in their houses, they (mostly women) spoke about the Saturday's meeting, Michelle's drawings, and who had said what during the class.

The classes went on for several weeks. Michelle brought a number of drawings with people working on tiny, individual parcels of land, then people gathered on the same land working the same earth. This led to ideas that we had hoped would be suggested. We were, however, happily surprised over who suggested them.

A small group of women, along with one man (our friend Chico Guzmán) came to our house one afternoon. "We want to start a chicken cooperative," said Clara, smiling. She then looked at Michelle. "We want you to help us organize it."

For the next few weeks Michelle visited the women in the barrio of Porvenir. They talked about logistics, how to get a cooperative formed, where to buy the chickens, who could build the chicken houses, how they would pay for the first bags of feed. Then the other inevitable questions: what will the local market vendors say when we start selling our eggs? Will they get angry with us? Will they try to do something to us?

"Let's worry about that when we get to it," said Clara. "It's going to take awhile to earn such problems."

The chicken cooperative did get off the ground. The women sold the eggs for reasonable prices and divided the gains among themselves. It became a small success story. Michelle and I had gradually learned something through the classes that we "taught": the drawings were a unique way of opening doors into the wisdom of the campesinos. She continued to use the drawings. People continued to argue and discuss and spend time together during the coffee breaks, sustaining the flow of questions and ideas that began each Saturday morning. I felt that Michelle and I had made a small breakthrough in our work. I strummed my guitar to gather the people together once again. I looked out at them as they sang along to a familiar tune and found their places in the circle of chairs. Then I sat down as Michelle hung another drawing up, one of a campesino working hard out in the fields, bent over under the hot sun; next to him a corpulent man with sunglasses is driving a shiny pickup truck; behind the pickup truck stand soldiers, their rifles dangling from their shoulders.

No one spoke. Pedro Lepe shifted from one foot to the next. Wicha's crossed arms fell to her lap. Somebody in the back of the room coughed. But no one said a word.

CHAPTER SEVEN

DAYS OFF

Panajachel is a place where gringos rest. Thus the town earned the nickname *Gringolandia*. It stands on the edge of Lake Atitlán, which is known as the origin of creation according to the great Maya book *Popul Vuh*. I stood upon the edge of the lake and watched the daily wave of fog roll from distant mountains and swallow the entire world before me. Within minutes the water and villages tapered upon its edges disappeared. Creation hid its treasure from the tourists for the rest of the day.

Most every foreigner who visits Guatemala ends up here. Missioners and other types of do-gooders are no exception. Many speak about Panajachel in inimical tones. We judge it for taking advantage of local indigenous customs and art so as to make a fast buck. Yet eventually we all show up.

Michelle and I took a few days off, drove south from Poptún for fourteen hours, and arrived at Atitlán's shore to celebrate our fifth wedding anniversary.

As the story goes, Panajachel was once an indigenous town, until about twenty years ago when an exodus of hippies left the United States in a search for the best marijuana grown in the hemisphere. Rumor brought them to Guatemala. I don't know if they found it, but they ran across something else just as lucrative: cheap land, along with an interesting native culture that proved to be marketable.

What once were the hippies of the sixties have become the yuppies and businessmen of the eighties and nineties. They are a distinct breed, looking much like the photos and films I've seen of Woodstock or of a college campus during the Vietnam protests—only older. In my naivete I thought they shared progressive ideologies, ones that promoted peace, working with the poor, social transformation, meatless meals, and the spiking of redwood trees. Not so. Most are capitalists to the bone. They buy up the Guatemalan clothes and flutes and coffee here at cheap prices, then sell them to the multitude of tourists who pass through town or package the products and send them to the States to be resold for dollars. They speak a strange Spanish, "*Ay hombre, estos hilos son los más* groovy *que he vendido!*" "Aw man, these threads are the grooviest I've ever sold."

Every day you wake up here to this strange mixture of people, dark-skinned Qàchiq'el Indians walking on the same streets where fifty-year-old hippies hang out, their long hair hanging off the edge of their bald spots like thin curtains.

In the afternoons we walked along the beach and watched as the mist and fog predictably swallowed the lake. We saw nothing of the small stores that stood fifty yards ahead of us. The mist swept through Gringolandia and swallowed the town's businesses, merchandise, the buying and selling of cultures.

On the day of our wedding anniversary we took a morning boat ride to the other side of Lake Atitlán and visited the room in which an Oklahoman priest named Stan Rother was murdered by Guatemalan soldiers in July, 1981. We sat in the room where he had been murdered. The local people had made it into a prayer room. In the church beside the rectory stood a jar filled with Father Rother's heart and other viscera. The mayordomos cared for the jar, one of their sacred possessions among a handful of reliquaries.

Outside of the church, on the streets of this village, stood the colors. The walking rainbows of Guatemala flung over the shoulders of Indians displayed only one reality. The faces themselves did not tell us their whole story. We were tourists, unknown, and not to be trusted. Behind us all walked those other colors. Green and brown camouflage tried to blend in with the crowd but could not, due to the cold, lithe metal hanging from their shoulders.

On our final morning in Panajachel I turned from my breakfast and caught the headlines of a newspaper. *Acribillados,* machine-gunned. Five farm workers were gunned down in Chimaltenango, a town we visited a couple of days ago.

"Yes, it's terrible," one of the waiters told us, "and no one knows who killed them. The army says it was the guerrillas, and the guerillas blame the army. Who knows?"

We returned to Guatemala City before heading back to

Poptún. In front of the missioner center house a crowd of people gathered around a dead vagabond. He had been shot and left in the street overnight. A mother with her children neared the scene, all of them with ice creams in their hands. They stretched their necks over the shoulders of the group, carefully balancing their cones as they stood on tiptoe.

CHAPTER EIGHT

BROTHER LEON

Brother Leon became a missioner decades ago. Like most people who join a mission group, he planned to live most of his life overseas. The religious institution had other plans for him. He spent most of his years tending the farm and cattle of his community in New York. It was not until he reached his late fifties that the mission group sent him to Guatemala.

Moving to Poptún, he followed the same rhythm of life that had been set for him in New York. He tends to the parish gardens. Stripped down to his waist, his once white shoulders have turned brown as earth. His wiry frame humbly betrays the weight of seventy years. He begins his day at six and ends it late at night, like the true Michigan farmer he is. In the evening he sits by the radio and listens to the BBC while winding fish string into tiny, perfect balls. "Sell 'em to the kids for a nickel apiece. They love it, go down to the river and such." Whatever money he makes off the fish line, he gives to the Catholic health program.

Leon also catches a variety of bugs and bottles them in alcohol. He sends shipments of fleas, butterflies, spiders, and cockroaches to companies in the States that turn around and sell them to high schools. He also gives this money to the health program. All the grasshoppers skewered to a cork backing and the tarantulas pinned to a block of wood in high school probably once lived happily in downtown Poptún years ago, before Leon sneaked behind them with his swift net.

"I do pretty well with the tarantulas. Everybody wants them, but they're hard to come by, at least around here. Not as many as in Flores up the road, no, not as many, but plenty of cockroaches around here, wow! You wouldn't believe how many I've sent up to the States. I sent about a thousand last month. Had them all stored up in my room. Finally got rid of them, but boy they're hard to keep, they'll crack all to pieces if you shake the bottle too much on these rough roads. You end up with cockroach crumbs. Hey, want a candy bar? The schools are more interested in different kinds of bugs, you know, the kinds you can't find in the States. They pay pretty good money for them, yessir. And the kids around here keep me busy. I offer them a nickel a bug, so you know they won't let me alone in the garden. Always coming up with a handful of 'em. I tell 'em I can't take 'em when they're crunched up, only whole."

Yesterday Leon and I drove to Machaquilaito to pick up a missioner health team that had wandered through the jungle for several weeks. The missioners had taught preventative medicine to a number of distant villages. No roads reached those communities. The only way in was by foot.

Leon and I drove five hours to the meeting place. He spoke to me all the way. I learned more about seeds and dirt and compost and possums that eat seeds and crows and plants than I have ever learned.

The Petén roads are similar to the ones used to film Jeep and Chevy truck commercials. Small boulders the size of footballs litter the way. Ditches, crevices, holes and gullies map the path. Such roads on a forty-five second commercial attract a certain romantic machismo. Not out here. My lower back, buttocks, and genitalia all suffered too many hours on these roads.

Leon defied the rocks that popped the truck into the air. He spoke through the pits that sent us both flying to the ceiling of the truck. I imagined that someone had taped a couple of pennies to the top of his needle on his record so as to ride the skips on the disc. It took little to keep him going, just my small responses ("Oh yeah?" "Really?" "What's a dandelion?" "How much alcohol?" "Where?" "How much for a tick?"). He kept the conversation streamlined, which kept me awake at the wheel.

When we arrived, we waited for only a short time before seeing the medical team walk out of the jungle. A woman named Jane led the way, her face burned from the sun. A smile broke forth as she saw the truck. Sheila followed behind, along with Domingo and Carmen, four weary, smiling faces approaching the Toyota as if it were a godsend of rest.

We had brought tamales wrapped up and packed in an icebox. We broke them open, along with clean water and some cheese. They dove into the food. While they rested against the truck's back door, Leon asked, "Sheila, bring me any bugs?"

"Only the ones that are still sucking my blood, Leon."

We piled into the truck. Jane drove, ready to hit the road. We talked, but Leon was suddenly silent. Too much of a crowd to squeeze a word in here and there. He kept his hands busy with breaking beans and sorting seeds.

We reached Poptún by sundown. They dropped me off at my house. I showered and prepared for an evening with Michelle. Mike and Carol DeVine had invited us out to their gringo farm. We spent the evening with the couple. Mike had known Leon ever since the elder missioner had arrived in Poptún. No surprise he had more stories to tell about the old man who would come to the gringo farm and catch butterflies while European tourists wandered about, wearing little and talking various languages.

CHAPTER NINE

WHEN THEY
KILL GRINGOS

June 9 was a Saturday morning. Michelle and I were up early, preparing for a morning meeting with some Church workers. At 7:00 Michelle answered a knock at the door. It was Carol DeVine and her teenage daughter María. "Hi, good morning, how's it going? Listen, I just wanted to tell you Mike's dead. He was murdered last night."

Carol and María entered. Carol's arms trembled as she reached toward the chair. She told us what she had recently learned. At 3:00 in the afternoon the previous day, Mike was driving his van from the center of town back to the farm. At a certain turn in the road, a white Toyota with no license plates, which had been parked there all day, forced him to back up. One of four men got in the van with him. Both vehicles pulled away. That night, Mike did not return home.

Carol asked for help from both the police and the local army base, but received none. As the countryside was impossible to search at night, people at the DeVine finca decided to wait until morning to go out and look for him. After searching for half an hour, the workers found the van off the road in the shade of some trees, untouched, with the keys still in the ignition. Mike lay behind the van. He had been decapitated.

Mike was killed in an obvious death squad fashion, chopped twice in the neck with a machete. They had tried to tie him, and it appears that he fought them off for a moment before one of the murderers came from behind him with the weapon. There are theories as to why, but no one really knows. No one speaks either, for we were in Guatemala. A black cloud of *desconfianza*, of deep mistrust, formed over the whole town. We felt it even among those who we counted as our friends. We became over-cautious, not wanting to say something wrong. As a friend warned us, "No one knows why Mike was killed, and you know, it's not even good to have an opinion."

During that week in June tension twisted into the stomachs of everyone we knew. The same Saturday that Mike was murdered, someone shot a man to death just behind the Catholic Church's parish hall. Though that murder seems to have nothing to do with Mike's death (the men had walked out of a bar together, just before one shot the other), it laced the black cloud of mistrust with heavier chains, pulling down tight a heavy, oppressive fear.

On the day they found Mike's body, Carol asked Michelle to stay with her. I ran around town with friends and family of the DeVines', trying to get hold of a coffin big enough to hold his body. In the hospital I was asked to accompany María, their daughter, as they prepared her father's body. There we stood, looking at the patched-up cadaver of the man who, the week previous, I had shared a beer with, had eaten supper at his table.

Doctor Morales, the head of the clinic, stood on the opposite side of the slab. Mike's body lay between us and the medic. "As you can see I did my best," explained Morales, almost angry, though I could not understand with whom. "I sewed it up completely," he pointed directly to the black crisscross over the pulled skin of the neck. "You wouldn't know it was severed if you couldn't see the string."

On Sunday most of Poptún showed up at the cemetery. He was a well-liked man, a quiet, shy farmer who apparently never got involved in anything controversial or political or any other words some used in order to rationalize their right to murder.

For weeks after the killing everyone went home long before nightfall. The first couple of weeks after the incident Michelle and I preferred to walk around together rather than separate. People double-locked their doors and kept a few lights on.

Two weeks after Mike's death a friend named don Pablo came to visit us. Don Pablo, 65, has white hair and a big, curly moustache that crosses over a lean, austere face. He has been a poor man all his life. As a Church worker he coordinated the Celebrations of the Word in the barrio named Ixobel. He was an old acquaintance of Mike DeVine. Mike had visited don Pablo through the years, helping the old man with his few farm animals. Don Pablo's daughters had all worked at the Finca Ixobel.

Don Pablo visited us Sunday afternoon. It was obvious that he was mulling something over. For over an hour and a half he talked, repeating many of the same circling phrases. "It's hard here, you know, life is very hard . . . the price of food, the rent of houses, everything is expensive. And no land, at least, not for the poor man . . . it's hard, here in this country. . . ." This went on for a long while. Both Michelle and I wondered to where it was leading. Soon he began to dig deep into the earth of his thoughts: He told us of his own history, how he had worked on agricultural cooperatives twenty-five years ago, how he along with other catechists farmed collective land so that everyone could eat, everyone could have their fair share. That is, until the army came around and started killing off his brother catechists at night. A wave of violence washed over the survivors and silenced them for the next quarter century.

"But it's hard to stay silent, don Marcos! Every time you open up the Bible, there it is before you: the challenge. The gospels speak of justice, rights, dignity for all. Jesus spoke of Life, the equality of people. But if you say that too loud here, you do not wake up the next day."

Don Pablo looked down at his hat on his lap with a sudden, intense sadness in his watery eyes. "Do you know how hard it is to read the gospels on Sunday to the people and give only *part* of the message? I don't feel like I'm completing it. There it is, clear and in front of us, and we can't complete the message. Not now. Not here. But there it is."

Twenty-five years of silence, like cold ashes, had been shovelled over him. But there remained the ember of an old fire, seeking out someone to rekindle it.

Days after Mike's death, I changed my running route. I used to run on the airstrip. Yet it became clear how isolated I was out there. Too easy to be lost, taken, abducted, and no one could hear your screams. I ran inside town, through streets where we have friends who see me pass by.

Rumors claimed that a group named the S-2 murdered Mike. They have been compared in structure to the United States' CIA. It is difficult to know anything or to verify such murmured statements. Enemies are never so clear, especially when they kiss and tell with supposed friends. Even Benedicto Lucas García, the well-known army chief of staff who controlled the military during the bloody years of the early eighties, was at Mike's wake and the funeral.* Gringo friends from Antigua, a small tourist town in the south, also attended. These North Americans opened up businesses in Guatemala years ago. Living in this country, they have done well for themselves. Like the army, they don't care much for the guerrilla movement, as guerrillas are bad for business. One of the gringos flung his arm around General Benedicto's shoulders during the wake. He said

---

*General Benedicto Lucas García was the Army Chief of Staff in the early 1980s. His brother, Fernando, was president. According to then Interior Minister Jaun José Roil Peralta, over 25,000 Guatemalans were murdered during the four years of the Lucas regime. According to one morgue pathologist, the floors filled with so many bodies, there was nowhere to walk. See Jean-Marie Simon, *Guatemala, Eternal Spring, Eternal Tyranny*, 1987. W. W. Norton and Company, p. 77.

to the rest of the crowd, "It's *this* guy who's gonna straighten out this country, clean things up. He's the next president of Guatemala, you can bet on that."

In town there was a rumor that the day before Mike was abducted, the market people passed the possibility of his murder from mouth to mouth. "They say they're going to kill the gringo today." That's how close it all gets to people: you have a cousin who is a cook in the army who heard about the plan to take the gringo, and your cousin mentions it to you at the dinner table. Being a lowly market vendor, there's little you can do. No one can do anything, except keep quiet, whisper the rumor, and hope it doesn't happen.

Three weeks after Mike's death Michelle and I argued. I wanted to take it easy for the afternoon, while she had to paint a sign for the parish. Chamba had asked her to make a "Welcome" sign for an upcoming church workshop. We also had to do some shopping since the shelves were getting low. To separate was the issue. We have not wanted to be outside of the other's sight since the murder.

While we fought, two young women from the barrio of Porvenir came by to visit. After they left, the one named María returned. With much shyness she asked if we would be the godparents for her son Jonathan. We said that we would love to, but that we could not oblige due to a policy that missioners could not promise to take on a commitment such as godparentship.

She shook her head in understanding. Then the tears came, along with the story. The man who left her pregnant five years ago took off with empty promises. Her son Jonathan was born in an unwanted shame. Perhaps the sponsoring of two Church workers, especially two gringos, could have cleaned him of that shame, and, in the eyes of the community, endorsed his goodness. Michelle held María and tried to press down her tears. I knew that she and I thought the same thing, that perhaps, to hell with the rules.

After María left again, Michelle and I made up, realizing this was not a great time to argue. She left to buy groceries. While she was gone our neighbor Sandra came by with her cute little terrorist of a daughter named Libne. Sandra was the wife of Dr. Pinto. She was known as a lady about town. She also had a way of dragging indigenous people through the mud with her discriminatory attitude. "If you ever have children, don't let an Indian look at them for too long," she once said to me. "His evil eye could make them sick and eventually kill them."

Not my idea of a pleasant visit. I hid in the back bedroom while Sandra screamed through the window, "Buenos días! Buenos días!" My toast began burning on the stove, sending smoke signals through the window. I would not move until she quit screaming "Good morning!" at the house.

At that moment a set of fighter jets circled over the town and roared over us three times, as if to compete with my neighbor who kept screaming, "Buenos días!" at my burning toast. I sat back in the dark of my bedroom, holding my breath, realizing, my God, it's only nine o'clock in the morning. . . .

Six hours later I made it to the little rest hut at the parish. I took a thirty-minute siesta in the hammock with a novel half-opened over my chest and a cool beer in my stomach. Half asleep,

I heard light footsteps upon the dusty floor. They approached me. I did not move, but opened one eye.

It was Father Chamba. Seeing I was asleep, he turned away. I told him to come on in. "I was just getting up."

He smiled, as if embarrassed. "I wanted to bother you with a favor." He told me the most recent story. Four Hondurans were being followed by a death squad called the G-2, which is made up of the Hacienda Police, the border patrol. The Hondurans were now in the Prince of Peace Church, holed up for the day. The men of the Squad were hanging out on the street in front of the church, waiting for them to come out. Chamba had tried to contact someone in the Human Rights Office in Flores (the capital of the Petén), with no luck. The phone lines were down. The whole town had been without outside communication for days, paradoxically enough, since Mike DeVine's death. Chamba had a mass to celebrate in a remote village. He asked if I could continue to call the Human Rights Office, just to see if there was any way of getting the men safely out of Poptún.

"Here, you may want this," he handed me a piece of paper where the man had scribbled the names of their families in Honduras, just so the families would know where their bodies were after the Squad got hold of them.

Rest days.

Michelle finished the sign that Father Chamba had asked her to make. He was planning a large meeting of Kekchi campesinos from all over the state. "Paint something, you know, welcoming," Chamba had said, moving his arms and hands about to demonstrate an abstract sense of hospitality. "You know. Something warm. Something that the Kekchi will understand. I don't know," he smiled at Michelle. "You're the artist. I'm just the guy with the ideas."

Michelle did paint something welcoming. In the midst of a gringo killing, and while Honduran civilians fled a death squad, Michelle took a large sheet of thick cloth, stretched it out over our cement kitchen floor, and began painting. She made long swipes of green that melted into a chest of red and a golden bird's face; she painted a sun coming from the lower left corner, its rays stretching into the large message written in two languages. The quetzal bird's long, flowing green feathers swooped a flight of liberation over the letters. Its blood-red chest expanded before the sun. The message was simple and to the point: *Okanqex Hilaanq B'a'yaq* in Kekchi; *Entren y descansen un poco* in Spanish.

Chamba was very pleased. He smiled up at the sign while a few local church workers placed it upon tall poles and wrapped banana leaves and bright green thatch around the poles and sign. "It's beautiful," he said. "How would you say that in English?"

Michelle quietly translated, "Come on in and rest awhile."

Chamba tried to say the English words. He laughed at himself. "I think I like it better in Kekchi." He touched Michelle on the shoulder, thanking her for her work. She smiled wearily. Then Chamba turned and opened his arms to the first people who were arriving for the meeting. He repeated to them all,

Okanqex Hilaanq B'a'yaq, repeating the message Michelle had painted: that other, indigenous side of Guatemala.

Yesterday we had a staff meeting, a gathering of all the local missioners. One among us had heard that an investigation was going on about Mike's murder. A secret agent walked around town in disguise, trying to pick up information wherever he could. Supposedly, the spy walked into a bar and began talking with some guy who shot pool and mumbled, "Yeah, they killed the gringo, and they're going to kill more gringos in town."

Our staff meeting turned dead silent. The only sound was that of the snapping beans between Brother Leon's calloused fingers. After a long moment Father Jim said to us all, "Well now, there's really no use worrying about it, don't you know. Just got to keep on living day to day." He pushed his arms in front of him as if to sweep away the weight of the dead air.

I could only half-appreciate Jim's sense of bravado. No one else moved. Just outside the room Guatemalan workers passed by. They glanced at the roomful of silent gringos who stared into the humid air among themselves.

While we met as a staff of missioners, Father Chamba had driven the Hondurans out of town. He took them to the border between Guatemala and Belize. The men walked over silently, after making sure the border patrol was nowhere to be seen. They disappeared to the other side, waving their thanks at the young Guatemalan curate. Chamba had come by our house to tell the story. He barely finished his beer when he stood up to leave. "Time to iron the bed sheets," he yawned.

After he left, Michelle and I crawled in bed together, not talking about anything, not even the meeting that morning over the news of the general threat upon all gringos. I turned off the light. Michelle kissed me goodnight.

A piece of metal whacked up against the front door.

The sound shot through the house like a rifle report. Michelle and I jumped onto each other and pushed our faces together. We held each other like a final protection as we waited for another whack against the door. Nothing followed.

The following morning I checked the door for marks. The old door wore a multitude of scars. It was difficult to distinguish which were old, which were more recent. I closed the door and came to the breakfast table. We had said nothing since the night previous. At breakfast Michelle asked, "Did you see anything?" a question that allowed us to speak. I suppose if she had not asked that, the subject would have never been brought up, as if it had never happened. We would have pretended that violence did not affect us, to the point of absurdly ignoring our fears while clinging to each other in a cold sweat and hiding under impotent bedsheets.

That morning I sat at my work desk and looked out the glassless window. I drank coffee and remembered the last time I had seen Mike Devine. He had driven by this same window. He had beeped his horn and had waved at me as he drove casually by. I waved back. I can still see the slight grin between his thick beard and moustache. It had been a lovely, sunny Friday afternoon, mere minutes before his death, a moment of salutation that could trick you into believing in human innocence. On June 29, 1996, just before going to press with this book, *The New York Times* reported on the findings of the presidential panel—

the Intelligence Oversight Board—which had begun an inquiry 15 months previous into several killings, including that of Mike DeVine. The article stated, in part, "The Central Intelligence Agency knowingly hired as paid informers a number of Guatemalan military officers suspected of political assassinations, extrajudicial killings, kidnapping and torture. . . . [The report stated] that several Guatemalan officers and officials who were paid informers for the C.I.A. covered up the military's role in the 1990 killing of an American citizen, Michael Devine."

CHAPTER TEN

THE CORN CHILDREN

"*Mario, ¿qué tal?*"

"*Bien bien.*"

"Mario, how's it going?"

"Fine, fine."

Mario always says he's *bien bien*.

"Hey Mario, you want to meet a friend of mine? Her name is doña Culebrita (Little Mrs. Snake)."

"Sure."

I pulled out the sock puppet from behind my back, changed my voice and moved doña Culebrita's mouth and red-button eyes before him. The four-year-old boy stared wide-eyed at the talking snake. He screamed, turned, and sprinted home to look for his mom. Tears streamed down his cheeks. Behind him ran his older sister Eva, repeating over and over again, "Don't worry Mario, it's only a sock, it's only a sock."

The next day Mario was more courageous. "And doña Culebrita?" he asked.

"Oh. She felt bad yesterday. She didn't mean to scare you."

"I wasn't scared."

"Oh. Well then." Out came doña Culebrita, along with four other puppets that Michelle and I made from scrap cloth, cardboard boxes, buttons. We used them as learning tools for the Church's adult formation groups. They were handy instruments for people who cannot read or write, yet who are eager to participate. During the classes the puppets triggered the men and women to speak up from the wisdom of their own experiences as people of struggling, poor communities. During the coffee break the children took their turn. Mario became good friends with doña Culebrita. He and Eva created their own puppet show while the adults ambled about drinking coffee.

Michelle and I spent a few minutes every day with children. While chatting with their parents about daily life, the children held onto our fingers and rode along, smiling at us, consuming the sudden attention from the gringo friends. They pulled forth our personalities: Michelle tended to give attention to the shyer kids, such as María Salome, who wore a rainbow of indigenous clothes and who spoke more Kekchi than Spanish. I moved more toward the rambunctious.

"Tell me the story about Paquito!" yelled Mario. "The one when Paquito tricks all the giants into knocking each other down you know yeah, that one." Mario's eyes opened wide as he imagined the three-headed giant. María Salome listened too, but she sat farther back, holding Michelle's fingers in her soft, earthy palm.

As they were the greatest blessing, so they too were the most tremendous loss. We visited the cemetery more than we wanted, mostly to bury people under the age of five. Poverty created the capricious rule "Survival of the fittest." Those not fit die to the legion of amoebas or parasites, to malaria, fevers, dengue, worms, measles, common colds, lack of food.

When a girl named Margarita died of a lung infection, I helped to prepare the body. I lifted her and placed the end of her five years in the sap-wet pine box. The movement tilted her head back and opened her throat. A final sigh left her. As I nailed, I remembered a favorite poet of mine, T. S. Eliot. I listened to his questioning words through the lense of these new experiences:

> were we lead all that way for
> Birth or Death? There was a Birth, certainly,
> We had evidence and no doubt. I had seen birth and
> death,
> But had thought they were different
> —T. S. Eliot, *Journey of the Magi*

They were always the smaller wakes, the less attended funerals. Their deaths are no surprise, not in Guatemala. The cold statistics about infant mortality rates that we read about in the States melted under the hot tears of a mother as the father put the tiny coffin on his back and carried his child down the road. Because it is so commonplace, mother, father, and child move down the street alone.

Manuel, a fellow church worker, nailed the lid to the coffin of his daughter as the family walked on ahead to church. Early this morning María Cristina dropped dead of a sudden fever. Yesterday she had been hanging on the knees of her father, begging him to play with her.

At the cemetery the hole had already been dug by friends. The family stood round. They were all Kekchi, so they had their own rite of burial. One of the elders held four candles in his hand, waiting to plant them after the hole was filled. Manuel had not cried one tear since this morning. The first shovel plunged into the loose earth, then tossed the clods into the hole. The dirt slapping against the coffin punched tears from Manuel's eyes. They wove silently over his cheeks as friends and family filled the grave with earth.

I looked around, staring at other sites in the cemetery, where I knew little bodies had been carefully placed. Realization covered me like a heavy mourning blanket: Michelle and I knew nine children here. Nine children in eleven months. By the end of our time in the country, that number would rise to seventeen. The reading of mortality rates did not prepare our hearts for all this.

After the hole was filled, the elder man planted the four candles in a square on the grave and lit them. The two that pointed east and west stood for the rising and setting of the sun, or as the Kekchi say, "The daily birth and death of God." The north and south candles burned away for the birth and death of human beings.

María Cristina's sun had risen, and now it had set, along with the light in her father's eyes.

On June 24 our first daughter was born. We named her Raquel del Carmen. Michelle and I argued over her name, whether to call her "Rachel" or "Raquel." "If we call her by the

Spanish, everyone will say, 'Ey, Raquel Welch!' I don't want my first daughter to be connected with a sex symbol."

I argued that such a thing would not happen, that the movie star was not as much in the limelight as before. "Who remembers Raquel Welch?" I asked her.

The following week we went to a regional church meeting. The bishop of the Petén attended. He was a small, stout man who wore glasses and whose whitening hair was cropped fairly short to his head. He always greeted people with a bear hug. When he saw Michelle and me, he made his huge grin even larger. He snatched us both up in his burly arms. I could feel his large metal cross dig into my ribs.

"And where is that girl of yours that I've heard about?"

We lifted her from a playpen and introduced her. He took her up in his arms. She stared up at him, as if unaccustomed to such large, grinning teeth.

"What's her name?" asked the bishop.

We told him.

"Ay! Raquel Welch! What a wonderful idea. You will be so beautiful, won't you, little lady? All the men will follow you . . . !"

I didn't dare look toward Michelle.

Raquel was born the summer of Mike Devine's death. One early morning I looked out a window of my home while Michelle and Raquel slept in our bed. I could hear Raquel's tiny snores, her breath escaping like sleeping bees. I watched the first rays of sun while drinking strong coffee. I think I may have prayed. I muttered a few meditations on this new concept called fatherhood. Yet I could not do so purely; the context of our lives snatched me up. We were no longer two, but three. There was another person to think about whenever making decisions. I would have grown weary with that thought, knowing how we had become accustomed to pondering over simple decisions such as whether or not to go to the store alone, whether or not to visit a nearby village. Then I turned and looked at the mosquito net that covered our bed, at the two sleeping faces of my family.

CHAPTER ELEVEN

SEX IN THE JUNGLE

Movies have a way of romanticizing certain experiences. Sex in the jungle is one. It's hot in the jungle, and humid. There are bugs everywhere, both inside and outside the house. The jungle also seems to attract all sorts of illnesses and physical limitations, everything from yeast infections to diarrhea to the crawling sensation of worms in your throat. It is quite a challenge to find a dry, quiet, bugless place within a pristine moment when you're not battling an infection or taking Flagil, a poison that rips the amoebas from your intestines like an inner blowtorch.

Still, sometimes such a magic moment did happen. Once we found it, Michelle and I thrashed underneath the mosquito net as if to rip it from the hook in the ceiling. Part of the energy came from pent-up libidos; the other part, however, seemed more frenetic, as if the tensions of strange murders and soldiers walking about outside our home had proved too much.

I could, in a limited manner, compare it to making love after drinking a full pot of coffee and consuming six chocolate bars on an empty stomach; though that too loses its metaphoric strength. Either way, weeks of abstinence (for all of the above health reasons), being new parents, and the psychological effects of organized violence sometimes could bring the sexual stress level to an interesting peak, enough to ignore the hot, still air of the night for a brief moment of exhaustion before slipping off each other's sweating skin.

I once made the mistake of dropping a used condom upon the concrete bedroom floor. Ecstasy has that effect on me. In the middle of the night I got up to use the bathroom. I lifted up the mosquito net and stepped down. A living mass moved over my foot and up to my knee. I scrambled to the lamp and flipped it on to witness ten thousand army ants, each the size of my thumbnail, covering my leg and moving like an ascending black curtain toward my (yes, naked) loins.

I jumped out of bed and put my other foot down. The floor crawled away. We evacuated the bedroom. I scraped the battalion of ants from my leg with the edge of my hands, then screamed toward the kitchen to collect my own arsenal: broom, mop, and a gallon of Clorox.

At the door I saw the reason for the invasion. A core of ants carried my spent condom upon their shoulders. I watched as the prophylactic disappeared under the door, followed by a multitude of sex-god worshippers. I was sure that my seed would be carried to a deep hole somewhere in a distant field. Poetry and symbolism had to be postponed for the moment, as the rest of the insect retinue still had to be dealt with.

I poured the Clorox over the cement floor, then cut a

swath through it with the broom. Michelle grabbed Raquel, then scooted our bed to one side as the wave of chlorine bleach washed over the multitude. What once appeared to be a thin, black, living bedsheet spread across the floor became a pile of war-dead. I scooped the glops of ant carcasses into the dust bin and tossed them outside. I turned and stood in a naked warrior-pose, with broom and dustpan in each hand and the empty Clorox bottle next to one foot. "It's safe now, honey."

Safe and sterilized. We could hardly go into our room now. The smell of the bleach ate at our nostrils. Yet no ant dared approach that now historic battlefield. We had to destroy that bedroom in order to save it. We slept in the kitchen. I had a restless set of dreams that played with various ideas of what a legion of ants would do with such a booty as the one they pulled through the crack in the door. My condom now possibly stood upon a pile of sacred sand where all the insects could come by and worship. Or perhaps it just filled a crack in an anthill's leaky ceiling.

CHAPTER TWELVE

WALKING TO LA MILPA

Don Chico Guzmán is a man of about forty years. He is a lean person with wild, curly hair sitting atop his head, and tiny threads of a moustache sprouting to the sides of his upper lip. His large, gentle eyes fall upon you along with a ready smile and laugh. He is a widower; his wife died of cancer a little over a year ago. He's been involved in the Church as a catechist for almost twenty years, though the past year he has pulled back to allow mourning to take its course. For several months he made a point of coming by our house once a week, just to chat and have some coffee.

About two weeks ago he invited me to see another part of Guatemala. "My milpa is really looking good now," he told us. "I'd like for you to see it, don Marcos. It's not that far away." He looked at me, and seeing that I am not made of the necessary stuff of rural struggle, said, "Well, we may want to drive in as far as possible. But you don't mind walking, do you?"

Such an invitation was not to be passed by. Chico's pride in his milpa, or cornfield, shone in his eyes. He did not own the land. He rented the four-acre square from a landowner. He was able to get it at a cheaper rate, due to its distance away from town. Though unlike the landowner, he did own the sweat and days that he had spent in that field.

I put on old clothes and slipped on some small rubber boots that covered my tennis shoes. "My God, don Marcos," he said to me on seeing the booties, "those won't last halfway there. There's a lot of mud between the road and my milpa. You sure you don't want my boots?" I assured him that no, I would be all right. A friend of mine from New York City had given me the booties for occasions such as this one. I was doing everything I could not to be an inconvenience. Pride came to the fore. I would show him that this half-gringo could take it, and with a smile.

We drove out early to the town of San Luis, about a half-hour from Poptún. On the other side of San Luis we hit more countryside, and drove to a spot on the edge of the forest.

In the jeep I got a lesson in Guatemalan perspectives. The privacy of the Nissan, the fact that only two people were in it (a luxury for most here), allowed for more honest words to flow out. Chico spoke of his perspectives on the guerrillas, on the army, on the situation in the country as a whole.

"Neither side is right, don Marcos, although one is worse than the other. The army, well, it's a given that they are diabolical. The guerrillas say they fight for the people. Perhaps they started that way. But the moment you put a gun in a man's hand, he feels a certain power. It goes to his head. The guerrillas become a political power of their own, and they lose sight of their vision and of the poor Guatemalans. We end up where we always were."

This conversation ended the moment Chico stepped out of the vehicle. "God, isn't it beautiful out here? I think you'll like my milpa."

We started walking. I immediately saw why Chico was worried about my rubber shoes. There stood a wide path before us, one that dropped down, then up again over the next hill. It disappeared into the mountains. The sun peeking over a cloud threw a glint upon the surface of the path, showing it to be pure mud.

"Now don Marcos, I know this road pretty well. You just follow me, and I'll step where I believe some rocks are hidden. That way you'll miss most of the mud. . . ."

As he spoke, I began to take control of my situation. I muttered to him, "You know, don Chico, it looks like that over there is much dryer than the middle of the path." I stepped into *over there*, all the way up to my crotch. I looked like a fallen flamingo yard decoration with one leg broken off. I grabbed hold of a jutting rock, tearing away at it with a silent, scarcely covered panic. I heard the mud, three feet down, suck away at my New York rubber.

"Ay, poor gringo."

Chico approached and helped me out. I'm still not sure how. My shoe appeared, but the rubber boot was gone, not to be seen until an archaeologist finds it in a few millennia.

"I can give you my boots," said Chico, "that's no problem at all."

"No! No, uh . . . I don't like boots anyway. I'll just go with my shoes."

"All right. . . ."

We moved on. This time the gringo followed every exact step the Chapín (or Guatemalan) took. Chico must have had X-ray vision. He stepped on stones that hid one inch under the mud.

We walked about four miles, up and down slippery hills, through forests that were more jungle than I anticipated. I fell several times. Though surrounded by mud, I managed to find stones with my knees, shoulders, elbows, and rump. When we reached the edge of his milpa, don Chico muttered, "There she is. Isn't she lovely?"

The milpa spread before us like a green blanket over one side of a jungle-surrounded hill. We lifted up one corner of that blanket and crawled inside.

"It goes up all the way to the malinche tree, then over to that side, where the tree line is, then, of course, right behind us. It's pretty big. I'm a blessed man. This corn will get us through the next four months. And it's good corn, healthy. God has blessed this earth, made it very fertile."

Get us through. Every one of them, Chico and his six children. The corn was almost ready for picking. In a few weeks he would harvest it and carry it out of the jungle on his back. Truck drivers would wait for him on the main road. He would throw it into their trucks, and a driver would pay him one-fifth of what he will sell it for in the market.

For now, Chico owned the moment. He now stood in

La Milpa. We walked through it. He periodically snapped ears from the stalks. "God, it's gorgeous! We'll take some back home, my sister will make us chuco, or perhaps tamales." He filled a sack with the pickings.

Chico took his machete and disappeared into the woods. I heard him hacking away at branches. He returned with an armful of wood and built a fire. Because of previous rain, the wood smouldered and tossed the smoke into our faces. Once it kindled, Chico leaned some ears—husks and all—atop the flames. Soon we ate roasted corn. The hard, roasted kernels popped off the cobs like toasted sugar. We stayed for a long while, squatting before the fire. We ate three *elotes* apiece, and laughed through mouthfuls of perfect food.

When we left he took the sack of picked corn and tossed it over his back. It threw him into campesino-position: *agachado*, stooped over, bent, looking straight down at the ground in front of his feet. He walked. That small, thin frame moved through the jungle, over rocks, balancing on skinny trunks that had fallen over rivers. He never slipped, as if adroit in his walking through poverty. I carried nothing, and believed that the jungle laughingly tossed me from side to side, bringing down the gringo with each fifth step.

Along the road Chico stopped and dropped his cargo. "You like avocados, don't you? Here's a whole tree ready to drop them all." I wiped sweat off my face with my T-shirt as he climbed the tree, using his feet as molded paddles against the trunk. I handed him a long pole that he had cut out of the forest. With it Chico knocked the fruits out of the branches. I ran from spot to spot, looking for them as they disappeared into the low growth of the forest.

We filled a second bag with avocados, much smaller than his of corn. "I will carry both bags, don Marcos."

"No way, don Chico, I'm at least carrying the avocados." Though proud, I knew my limitations. Though much bigger than Chico, that sack of corn would sink me into the bowels of the jungle, and that would have been hard to explain to Michelle. I threw the sack of avocados onto my back. We continued on our way, with Chico shaking his head and quietly chuckling.

The weight of the avocados acted as a balast, and sank my feet into the mud. Forty minutes later we arrived at the jeep. We threw our haul into the back. Chico laughed at me, "Ay, doña Michelle will have my hide. Look at her man," and he gestured to my body-coat of mud.

"This is exactly how I want to be."

"You didn't mind that, did you? I mean, you seemed to like it. Maybe, someday, you'll make a farmer yet." He laughed. "But farmers don't come out of the jungle looking like piglets."

We drove home, covering the seats of the Nissan brown. Michelle greeted us at the door, but stepped back as we walked in. Later that night, after baths, we gathered in Chico's one-room house and drank *chuco*, a drink of hot cornmeal and sugar. We laughed about the day and the slippery Dance of the Maladroits that I learned as we walked to La Milpa.

CHAPTER THIRTEEN

TWO CHAPINES,
ONE GUANACA*

Michelle, Raquel, and I attended a special mass one Wednesday morning, celebrating the fiftieth wedding anniversary of Mr. and Mrs. Paco and Romelia Valle. Half a century ago the Valles came to Poptún when it was but a tiny village of huts scattered around the same area of jungle. Now they were well-established, and like Abraham and Sarah, they left a lineage that matches the number of stars in the sky. The whole center of town is composed of Valles, all of them their children. Around the town square every home ends in their name.

We sat among some Valle children, grandchildren, and great-grandchildren. They brought out bottles of colas and rum, the common drink among celebrating Chapines. We toasted and talked. Michelle and I began to better understand family

*Chapín is the nickname for a Guatemalan. A Guanaco is a Salvadoran.

connections ("Oh, so *you're* Señor Valle's first son . . . and you've just been elected mayor of Poptún. Isn't that something. Congratulations!").

About two drinks into the celebration a middle-aged, robust man with stylish wire-rimmed glasses sat down before us, smiling as he reached for the rum. In the party's din I could barely hear him as he shook our hands. Marimba music beat from behind as we began a casual conversation. "Gosh, I'm tired these days," he told us while mixing rum and cola, "but I hope to get some rest, now that I'm out of politics."

I looked over the rim of my glass and realized who he was. Done with politics. I had seen his face before in the national papers. He recently ran for President of Guatemala and lost. Thus, he had come home to the Petén. His name was Benedicto Lucas García. He was known as *El General.* He had been the Minister of Defense for Guatemala in the early eighties, known as the crimson years. While he was in command, approximately 27,000 Guatemalans, most of them indigenous, were either tortured, murdered, or both. During that time, the army systematically burned villages, kidnapped young men, built torture centers, and blanketed the country in a national fear.

Little Poptún is his hometown.

Michelle also realized who he was. "We better get home now," she leaned over and whispered.

"But the food is coming," I balked.

"Eat fast."

We tried eating fast, which was difficult with Raquel who had just begun the grabbing stage, and who methodically placed tamale pieces all over her mother's dress. Meanwhile, Lucas leaned over the plate of his little grandson, who looked up at his grandfather with soft eyes as the man meticulously sliced up the tamale for the boy, smiling, the essence of fatherly patience. His side of the table contrasted sharply with our tamale-flinging.

Every few minutes someone approached Lucas, offered him a handshake or an embrace, all of them greeting him, "My General, how are you? My General, so good of you to come." Señor Valle's son forced himself to approach the retired minister, nervously embracing him, as they were not of the same political party. The two men standing behind the General wore sunglasses. They turned their heads right and left like good bodyguards. Landowners and peasants alike walked up to him as if to kiss the ring and receive the blessing of an archbishop. Yet they were tremulous greetings, ones that emanated with a surviving attitude, *Better to be on my General's good side, so as not to be on his bad.*

Michelle and I stood to leave, wiping tamale debris off Raquel's smiling face and our shirts. We shook everyone's hand, including his. "I pray you may have a happy afternoon," he smiled, formal and sincere, standing among the other Poptunecos, one of their own. He seemed almost handsome were it not for history blotting his soul. Yet he was, indeed, the perfect gentleman.

They murdered our gardener last week.

Joaquín Che' Ax, a Kekchi indigenous man of fifty years, used to come to our house every three weeks or so to clean out the weeds and wild shrubs that grow in our backyard. He would work two days, chopping low to the ground with his machete. He spoke little Spanish, but that did not keep us from chatting during break time, when Michelle or I brought him a cool drink and sweet bread.

Two months ago Joaquín suffered a stroke that left him almost speechless, even in his native language. Like many stroke victims, he fell easily to sudden tears, to forgetfulness and constant disorientation. At times he would walk out of the house and wander around the neighborhoods until his wife María came after him.

One Thursday afternoon he mumbled aloud, "Lookin' for don Marcos . . . he give work." He took off. María and her children spent the afternoon searching. He never arrived at our house. Some folks said they saw him in Santa Fe, a neighborhood' way on the other end of town.

As night came on, he still did not appear. Roberto, Joaquín's son, and I drove around at 10:00 that evening, searching in complete vain, as there were no lights outside of town. All we could see was the shaft of earth before us, cut open with the light of my vehicle. After about an hour we decided to turn around and head back.

The afternoon of the following day Michelle came home early from a church meeting and looked straight at me. "He's dead."

Lo mataron, They killed him, is the common phrase used in Guatemala whenever someone is murdered. The unidentified pronoun *They* seems the best way to express the unknown entity that takes wandering victims such as Joaquín. While buying the coffin, then dressing his body, I saw the work that *They* did. As Joaquín's cousin and I peeled off Joaquín's shirt, his cold arm slapped against my chest. I saw the circle of bruises around his wrist. "Good Lord," I muttered, "it looks like they tied him."

"They did," said the cousin, "they tied his hands and feet, then beat him before shooting him."

With his shirt off it was easy to see the bullet wound: one shot half an inch from the central thorax, perfectly piercing the heart. I looked at his eyes, and there I saw Joaquín for the final time, silent, wearing the face of graveyard peace. Then the smell took over, that of raw chicken sitting out in the sun too long. The first hours of decay force the living to quickly bury the beloved dead. Though growing accustomed to the stench, we dressed him swiftly and placed him in his pine box.

We dug the hole that evening. People questioned who would have committed such an atrocity, tying and killing a poor sick man like Joaquín. After some investigation it was believed that either thieves or hoodlums were guilty, making a victim of someone wandering about. No one really knew, nor would we ever find out. Joaquín became but a number, one forgotten Guatemalan Indian among a lost multitude.

I slept in one morning. Michelle answered the knock at the door. She came and sat by the side of the bed and put her hand on my shoulder. "Honey, wake up. I'm afraid I've got some bad news. Your grandmother died last night."

It was no surprise. Romilia had been sick for a long time. It did, however, bring a heaviness upon me as I crawled out of bed and began the day. First I thought of my mother who had taken care of *abuelita* for these past few years. Romilia suffered from Alzheimer's, a slow, sad disease that drains the children as much as the sick person. Four years ago she began forgetting everyone's names. She gradually descended into the decrepitude of a tiny body. My mother was with her all the while, feeding her, bathing her, talking with her in Spanish as if trying to reach back into some recess of memory, groping to find her mom. Soon she understood the impossibility of such endeavors, and she took the long road to acceptance. "I've been mourning for some time now, Marquitos," Mom told me over the phone. "It's sad. But there's also a certain peace with her death."

Letting go. More difficult than grasping. I held onto memory, to that woman Romilia, she who was one of the main influences of my being in Central America. I looked upon her as the great reminder that I am *guanaco*, or Salvadoran. She was the matriarch of my bloodline. Before her sickness I spoke to her in Spanish, and she told me the old stories of her husbands (three of them, all who died long before her), her children, the old country, and the visions she saw while she slept. I took her stories and wove a novel from their tattered threads.* I knew then I had entered into her world of Latin America. She had gifted it to me. This is how I will remember her: sitting in the kitchen with a burning Lucky Strike between her fingers and having an occasional shot of whiskey before her as she spread the old stories of life in El Salvador upon the kitchen table.

I awoke and crawled out of our bed here in this small town of Central America as my family placed *abuelita* in a sepulchre in San Francisco, California. I made coffee and poured myself

---

*A Fire in the Earth, 1996 Arte Pùblico (Houston).

a cup. Then I reached down and grabbed our daughter, held her to my neck and whispered, "*Ay Raquelita, te quiero tanto.*" ("I love you so much, girl.")

It was then that the tears came, not so much for grandmamá as for myself. She who wove me into the cloth of this land was now gone. But she had left me the stories, and I held them in a kitchen full of memories.

CHAPTER FOURTEEN

FREEDOM AND CONTROL

Michelle visited a nearby village named Machaquilá. She had asked a friend to accompany her, but at the last minute the lady had to cancel. Michelle took off alone, driving out of Poptún to attend a celebration of the Word with some local church people. Though we prefer never to travel alone, Machaquilá was not far away. Little could happen during such a short trip.

On the outskirts of town the police stopped her. She thought little more of this than the usual fearful question of why in the world are they stopping people these days? Other cars before her had been detained, their papers checked, then waved on. Michelle handed the officer her truck papers and her license. They looked at it a good long time, then waved her on. She geared into first and took the dusty, rocky road to Machaquilá.

At the end of the celebration, Michelle stood up with a few announcements from the parish house, then asked if anyone needed a ride into Poptún to do some shopping or run errands. Probably for the first time in the history of Guatemala, no one needed a ride into town. She climbed back into the truck and, waving goodbye, drove off.

The policemen still stood at their little post on top of the hill. Other cars were being stopped. Michelle thought that since they checked her just two hours previous, they would wave her through. A small car slowed down ahead of her, ready to be checked. When the first cop spotted Michelle's jeep, he waved the little car on, disinterested. Then he stopped Michelle.

No cars stood behind her. All the vehicles ahead had driven away. No buildings, no houses, not even a wind to make noise. Only countryside, this Toyota, and the police. The one cop came to the driver's window. "Let's see your papers."

"I just showed them to you hardly two hours ago," Michelle said, though she reached for the glove compartment. While she talked, four other policemen left the little building post and walked toward the Toyota. They surrounded it, one in the front, two on the passenger side, one in the back. In total five policemen stood around her with automatic rifles in hands. The ones to each side opened all four doors. They leaned in and breathed on her.

"Give us a ride into town."

She does not know how long, but a silence fell upon them all. She struggled through an enwrapping fear as she looked for some response that would be acceptable, given the situation.

"Come on. We want a ride."

Too many things came down upon her, too many people: the face of Sister Dianna Ortiz, the U.S. woman who had been kidnapped by the police, then taken to a torture center; the faces of Mike DeVine and Joaquín Che' Ax; all of them real, legitimate and deadly warnings.

They continued to demand that they be allowed in the truck with her. One made a move to get in the vehicle. A response rose out of Michelle's gut and fell over her lips, "I'm sorry, but I work for the diocese, and our Bishop does not allow us to give rides to people who carry guns."

"¡Ah, la gran chingada!" ("Oh, fuck this!") yelled the first one. He grumbled something to his companions, which made them slam close all four doors. "Go on, get out of here," said the first one, waving his arm toward Poptún.

Michelle drove home, billowing dust behind and wiping tears off her cheeks. She stumbled through the door of our house and fell before the rocking chair where Raquel and I sat. The story tumbled from her all at once, pushed out with the fear only a woman can know.

I was amazed that Michelle thought so quickly and said what she did about the Bishop. It was no lie: the Bishop does not want his missioners to give rides to armed people, soldiers, guerrillas, or police. But in saying that, she also stated that she was a church worker. This forced the police to consider the political pull that the Church has in the country. Whatever they were planning to do, the officers decided it was not worth the risk.

Baby Raquel opened doors for us in ways that we never imagined. Right here in our neighborhood, as a matter of fact, starting with doña Olivia.

We have bought tortillas from Oli since the day that we moved into our house. Every day at noon Michelle or I walk to her house about three doors down from ours and bring home a towel full of hot, fresh corn tortillas.

One day we were stretched for work. Both Michelle and I had to be at a meeting together, and it would have been difficult to bring Raquel along. Oli offered to take care of her. Oli's house quickly became Raquel's second home.

When Raquel was first born, Michelle and I decided that there was no way we were going to have anyone else clean our clothes for us (even though employing others to clean your laundry is very common here, and it is a great source of work for many folks). I suppose that was the gringoness coming out of us. It did not last long. In the first week we spent every hour of the day washing, making meals, and cleaning load after load of diapers. We washed all our clothes by hand in the *pila*, the large, cement, all-purpose sink; our resolve quietly melted. We broke down and checked out the neighborhood to see if there was anyone who did other people's laundry as a source of income. We found out that our tortilla woman also washed clothes for a number of households, and that Oli was willing to take on more.

Only one person questioned this: Father Jim. When I mentioned to him our new setup, he was chagrined.

"Your tortilla woman also is your diaper woman? My friend, do you know how tortillas are made?"

"Sure. By hand. Why?"

"Just think about it. And don't ever invite me over for lunch."

I disregarded this as unnecessary information. Oli became a grandmother figure to Raquel. "Look at the present little Raquelita gave me," smiled Oli one afternoon when I came to pick the girl up. I looked over at the wall, where a hunk of wall paper had been torn off the wood beams. I felt terrible about this, but Oli only laughed. When we returned a few days later, the rip was still there, untouched. *Es mi recuerdo*, laughed Oli. "My memento from the little one."

We have become accustomed to the fact that in most of the meetings we facilitate, at least two *orejas*, or ears, are present. They are called the *comisionados*, or commissioners. They receive a stipend from the army in return for listening and watching what is going on, and for reporting any anomalies to the local military base.

What I find strange is that some of the fellows are actually good men. A number of them are church leaders in their local communities. I don't know if some of them take the job voluntarily, or if they are pressured to do it. Either way, Michelle and I try to be careful, forming our statements adroitly so as to say nothing that could be taken as a threat to the status quo. However, in this work, we end up talking about the daily realities and what to do about them.

In one of the meetings, in which about forty men and women gather, we usually break into small groups and discuss a few verses from scripture. The conversations usually end up as practical interpretations of the Gospels, that is, what do the Gospels have to say about our way of life, our present-day struggle? This is exciting, as the discussions usually move toward issues such as lack of health care, lack of schooling, the fact that no one owns any land, etc. I am not sure how the *comisionados* feel about such dialogues.

Then Chico, one of our closer friends here, informed us of another reality. "Yes, don Marcos, there are the comisionados. But you do know, don't you, that there are other *orejas* in the room too? They are the unofficial ears, those who sit even more quietly than the officials. They are the ones you have to be really careful about. They are the ones who are really in control."

Pilar Martín Perez was one of the more beautiful storms to pass through Poptún. She was a lay missioner like ourselves, but her home *patria* was Spain. She had moved to Poptún a couple of years before we did, working in the Catholic formation center on the other side of town. Most of her work dealt with ongoing formation for the catechists, the lay people who worked for the Church in their local communities.

After our daughter was born we had more chances to see her. She flew by the house whenever she could so as to plant a thick, wet kiss on Raquel's cheek.

"Hello, hello, hello, how are all of you?" Pilar rolled her Castilian Spanish through the hallway before her as she turned the corner and grabbed me and Michelle around the waist to kiss us. "Now where is the little one? Raquelita, it's time to play!"

"Well, uh, she may be asleep, Pilar . . ." muttered Michelle.

"Oh, no time for that, come here, little girl," she smiled while leaning over and grabbing Raquel from the crib.

Raquel grinned confusedly, blinking awake, while Pilar squeezed love into her.

"Well, I must go. I was just heading out to Achotal and thought I would stop by and pinch the little lady," and pinch she did. Once again, kisses given, Pilar marched out the door, with a wind swallowing up her path.

At parties Pilar was always coaxed to stand up before us and sing *la jota*, a style of Spanish song typical to her country. I never knew the history of the *jota*. All I knew was that when Pilar stood to sing it, placing her hands on her hips and thrusting one shoulder and her chest before her, a perfectly toned voice penetrated you to your loins, a warm sensuality filled the room with that mellifluous Castilian cry. She held you aloft with that song, and when she ended it, you knew she could drop you where you stood. And you wouldn't mind.

At 3:30 this morning shots exploded in front of our house. Though they woke me, I knew not to be afraid. I could tell they were not gunshots nor bombs (you get good at distinguishing after awhile). They were fireworks, and they were in my honor. The firecrackers rattled off right below the front of our window. After the last cracker, out of the sudden silence rose the voices of several young people, "*Estas son las mañanitas que cantaban al rey David. . . .*" "These are the morning psalms that they used to sing to King David. . . ."

In honor of my birthday. It is tradition in Guatemala to light firecrackers near the house of a birthday person before the sun rises, then to sing them the sweet song of *Las Mañanitas*, the early morning tune. I jumped out of bed, tossed the mosquito net to one side and ran to the door. Eight teenagers from a nearby barrio stood outside. Orlando, a young man of twenty years, played guitar behind them.

We opened the door and welcomed them in. Michelle made coffee and arranged sweet bread on a plate. Raquel, not used to waking up at 4:00 A.M., cried as she stared at all the people in her front room. She settled down into my arms as the teenagers continued playing music and singing other songs. Don Pedro, an elder catechist from Porvenir, chaperoned them. With little coercion he told a couple of stories. Don Pedro's ostensible shyness blew off him with a sneeze.

"Once there was a catechist who was such a lousy preacher that one evening, while he preached, the people got fed up with him and ran him out of town. They promised that, when they caught him, they would just kill him for being such a lousy homilist. Well, this poor catechist ran into the forest and, seeing that they were gonna find him sure as anything, dove into a shallow cave on one side of the hill. Unfortunately, the cave had no other outlet, so if they found him, he could not escape. They would have just trampled him into the cave's wall. 'Ay God,' prayed the shaking catechist, 'if you would only hide me in some way. Send a huge wall to cover the hole of the cave so as to hide me.' At that moment a *wee* little spider dropped down on its string toward the catechist, then began weaving a web right there at the door of the little cave. 'Son of a bitch,' says the catechist, 'I ask for a great wall, and all you do is send me a spider?'

"The spider kept weaving, until she finished her beautiful web right over the catechist's head. It connected to all sides of the cave's mouth. When the people came, with clubs in their hands, they looked all around. 'Anybody see him?' 'No,' said another. 'What about that cave? He could be in there.' 'Impossible,' said the one just above the catechist, peering down into the darkness, 'there's a cobweb here, he would have had to break the web in order to get in. Let's move on.' And the angry congregation went away. The preacher then knew that God had sent him a great wall, in the form of a tiny web. The moral of the story: If you're a lousy preacher, don't get in front of an angry crowd."

The group visited for about an hour, drinking coffee and eating sweet bread. They played more music. As the sun rose they moved on. We waved to them as they walked down the dirt road, Orlando still playing *La Bamba* softly on the guitar.

I taught a confirmation class to teenagers for several weeks. Much of our work has dealt with adults. To teach confirmation to teenagers is a unique challenge. There were about seventy kids wanting to get confirmed. Surprisingly, everyone showed up.

My subject was the Old Testament, which is my favorite part of the Bible, as it has the most interesting and dramatic stories (I must confess, I probably get more into the literary aspect of the text). We recently covered the Exodus story, specifically the flight out of Egypt and the persecution of the people of Israel.

We met in the church, filling up the first several pews. I lectured from up front, down from the altar. The kids all stared at me, barely noticing a sudden hesitation in my voice. I kept speaking, though a Kaibil had just walked into the church. The Special Forces soldier did not genuflect. He only stared at me all the way to the pew where he sat, right among the teenagers.

I froze up inside, but kept on going with the class. I became acutely aware of what I was teaching: Exodus. In the circles I've worked in, there's no getting around the fact that Exodus is the story of an oppressed people struggling for their liberation. Not popular material among the army here.

Nerves began to pick at me, along with an anger that kept me teaching. I could not help but notice the Kaibil: he wasn't a foot soldier, but a decorated man, perhaps a lieutenant. All he did was stare at me for a full twenty minutes. Then, as if hearing enough, he stood and walked out.

After the class I ran to the parish house and looked for Father Chamba. He was taking the Sunday afternoon off, swinging in the hammock that hung in the champa. A beer stood on a chair to one side. "Marquitos!" he smiled, "How's the class going?"

"Fine, I think. But I've got a question, and I want your opinion." I told him what happened. Chamba's smile dropped quickly when I mentioned the feared name "Kaibil." He listened intently. Then his face changed into understanding, as if he had heard this before, plugging my experience into the recesses of Guatemalan history.

"They've been known to do that. They used to do it more often a few years ago. Maybe they're picking up old habits. They also carry in tiny tape recorders in order to record what you are saying to the people. But more than anything it's just a blatant reminder that they're the bastards who are in charge, and that they don't want us to forget it." He paused as if to think, then asked, "What was it you were covering today?"

"Exodus, the first chapters."

"Oh shit. You okay?"

"Yeah. But could you loan me a clean pair of pants?"

We discussed the issue for a few minutes more. I mounted my bike and quickly pedaled home. I waited a few hours before telling Michelle. I thought about not telling her; but we've never worked that way.

I walked to doña Oli's house this afternoon for tortillas. As always, I knocked. "Come on in," called Reina, one of Oli's daughters. I stepped into the parlor.

"Come on back for goodness sake, don Marcos. You are so formal when you come into our home," laughed doña Oli. I smiled and walked back into the kitchen, where Oli and her two teenage daughters were busy patting tortillas on the large, hot comal (hot plate).

"I suppose my mother taught me that, to not go into someone's home unless you're invited."

Oli stared at me, herself looking like a reprimanding mother. "Yes, but what did your mom say about friends' homes?" She handed me a hot tortilla with some cheese on it while I sat down on a stool. "Besides, this is the way good neighborhood gossip is collected," and Oli laughed while she flipped a tortilla with her calloused fingers.

I ate and watched them as they worked. We talked, passing the time as they stacked a dozen tortillas into the towel I had brought with me. It is in such moments that I learn, once again, that cultural differences are as subtle as a breath. Then again, perhaps there are not too many distinctions between this lifestyle and that of the Southern U.S., where "down-home hospitality" is a norm. I've noticed that in either culture, to rush into someone's life is seen as rude. It also means you probably won't come out with what you wanted. It's in moments like the one in Oli's kitchen that the stuff of friendship is made.

Father Chamba walked into our kitchen and threw his backpack onto the table. "I need a drink."

I knew that he knew that I had a bottle of Johnnie Walker. I found it in my closet and pulled out three small glasses. Michelle and I sat down with Chamba. I poured some into his glass, then made to pour into my own. Chamba looked up at me and wearily chuckled, "I didn't say 'when.'" I gave him some more.

"What's the matter?" I asked.

"I'm not sure where to start."

"How about the beginning?" Michelle said.

He told us the story as we sipped our whiskey. He had been gone for several days, having visited tiny villages on the edges of the state. He had visited a hamlet whose name is one of those multi-syllabic Kekchi words that my torpid, bilingual mind has problems digesting. "I had never been there before. They knew I was coming. They had this huge arch made out of bamboo and thatch, my God, I felt like the Bishop riding into town. They had not celebrated a mass out there for years. I was worn out, but I was also glad to see them. The joy on their faces," Chamba raised up his hands as he spoke, "it was just incredible. It's in such moments that I feel like this job as a priest has some relevance. I got down from my mule. They watered the animal, then watered me: they gave me some cocoa and a hammock to rest in. I was lying there as relaxed as you could ever imagine, talking with the elders about the weather and the land. It was wonderful. Then the elders changed the subject."

Chamba drank the scotch. He looked at each of us. Michelle bent into the table. She twitched at a lock of her blonde hair, as she always does whenever nervous.

"These elders," explained Chamba, his voice slightly rattled, "they said to me, 'Father, it is so good that you have come so far to visit us. We are blessed with your presence. We have only one little favor to ask of you. The last priest who came through here brought those funny looking little pieces of white crackers and that wine to use for the mass. We were wondering if, this time, we could use something, you know, different.'

"Then they showed me what they meant by different. They moved out of the way. I lifted up slightly from my hammock. My heart was already racing, because I had a suspicion . . . and damned if my suspicion wasn't right. There, right in front of me, sat two huge cauldrons of tamales and three pots of hot chocolate."

I know that my eyes opened wide, because I felt my left contact shift. I said nothing, but I'm sure a gasp escaped me. Chamba drank. I turned to Michelle. She stopped twitching her hair. Her face fell slightly, as if disappointed.

"What?" she said. "What's the problem?"

"Don't you see?" said Chamba, his hand stretching over

the table. "They wanted me to bless the tamales and the hot chocolate into the body and blood of Jesus Christ!"

"Oh, Wow," she said. "That's neat."

Both Chamba and I responded in chorus: "NEAT?"

Chamba was a priest. I had been in seminary for two years (before being rescued from that fate by Michelle). Both of us men understood the depth of the crisis. Still, the fear on our faces did not seem to sink into Michelle's comprehension.

"Honey, the Eucharist is the backbone of the Church," I explained. "It's not something you mess with. I remember one of my teachers in seminary saying 'What do you want, priests blessing Coca Cola and Doritos into Jesus?' I mean, I know it's not the same thing . . ."

Michelle reminded us of what we all knew. "Of course it's not the same thing. Aren't tamales and cocoa sacred foods for the Maya?"

Chamba shook his head affirmatively, "That's my point. You see, I don't have any problem with the concept. I mean, I think that's how it should be. In fact, I've said that before in Church meetings: the local people should have the freedom to express their faith with their local symbols. You know, take control of their own lives, even in how they worship. But this is the first time I ever had to make a decision about it . . . My balls could be in a sling if this ever got out."

"With whom?" asked Michelle.

Again, incredulity streaked over Chamba's face. "With everybody. The Bishop. The Archbishop. The Cardinal. The Pope."

"Aw, forget all them," she said, laughing. "This is the nineties."

Neither Chamba nor I understood what that meant.

"So," asked Michelle, "did you do it?"

Chamba mumbled something, but it was neither Kekchi nor Spanish. It was no language I had ever heard.

"Come on Chamba, what happened?" I asked, suddenly enjoying the fact that the bravest man I have ever met, one who has challenged landowners and soldiers alike, was scared shitless over an ecclesial rule. "Did Jesus become a corn man?"

Again, Chamba said nothing. He looked down at the table, drank from his glass, and looked about for the bottle. We egged him on, urging him to tell us, but he never said.

CHAPTER 15

ACQUIRING THE TASTE FOR DEATH

They are ubiquitous. The old Blue Bird school buses, bought cheap across the border, held together with new coats of bright colors. Various destinations are written across their foreheads: Sanarate, Poptún, Puerto Barrios, Río Dulce, Santa Elena, Zacapa, Belize. At some point the privately owned jalopies will go to Guatemala City, as everyone in the country, for one reason or another, travels to the capital.

These ramshackle bus lines run through the nation like intravenous drops of transport, with passengers crammed into every crack of space. Others hang out of the doors, while a few always ride on the roof, clutching the iron luggage rack. As few people own cars, such repainted rust heaps are their only means of transportation. Yet no one likes to board them, as there are too many stories of bus wrecks, flipping over a ridge in the Petén, running into another bus in Zacapa. The owners of the bus lines are infamous for not spending money on necessary parts and ordering their drivers to make twenty-four hour runs. It's common to see a driver pull into Poptún from Guatemala City—an eight to twelve hour trip, depending on the rain—eat a meal, then crawl into the empty bus to sleep until 4:00 A.M., when the early morning passengers tap at his window, ready to go to the capital. The driver cannot complain; asking for better work conditions means losing a job. And the owners of the lines, obvious to all, have been snatched up by that old-fashioned demon called greed, as he sees the bills roll out of the hands of those in need of transport. Such scenarios lead to inevitable endings.

We drove from Poptún to the capital, already weary from the day, the heat, the rocky, mud-covered Petén road. Now we drove on asphalt. Only thirty more kilometers stood between us and Guatemala City. Raquel slept in her car seat. Michelle and a visiting friend, a young fellow named Paul who is a professional photographer, chatted over the front seat while I stared listlessly at the curvy road ahead. So accustomed was I to seeing old, wrecked school bus shells that I took no notice of the one flipped over on its side on the curve ahead of us. It rested silent, unmoving, apparently abandoned. Paul did not live here, and such a sight caught him. "Gosh, that looks terrible. I wonder when it happened?"

"Hard to tell, maybe a few days ago—" But I was quickly corrected by the head of a man that popped through a shattered window. His shoulders and trembling arms followed.

He lifted himself out as Michelle yelled, "My God, no, it just happened, it's happening!"

Though the bus lay dead on its side, the chassis dangled in the air. The transmission, axle, and tires hovered over the highway as if a giant cheese cutter had run through the vehicle in mid-flight, ripping the base from the passenger load.

I drove aside it, then pulled up ahead and parked the jeep. The first ones to arrive, we jumped out to a legion of trapped screams. As we ran to the old school bus, I saw nothing but a pile of distorted legs, arms, and faces, all beating against one another and against the twisted metal bondage. The bus had skidded onto the door side, where the first few to have escaped now reached into the bulk of flapping appendages. Diesel belched forth from the engine onto the leg of a young girl pinned under the door. Hands reached out through the broken glass, and the faces, all smashed together and wrapped around shards of metal, screamed at me like Picasso's *Guernica*. I stopped, impotently staring at it all, until the man who escaped first screamed at me. "Hurry up, we've got to get them out!"

We pulled at the ones we could reach, those not completely wedged in. With help, the teenage girl bathed in diesel wriggled out from under the door. I carried her away as she beat against my chest and arms as if still trapped under the bus, and she cried for her mother and father who were still inside.

One by one the quivering legs and arms untied. The crimson stained bodies sluffed away, shocked at their ability to walk and breathe. Other travelers stopped to help. Michelle drove ahead to a hotel and called for ambulances. It was 3:30 P.M. when she put the call in.

Within twenty minutes we pulled out the few remaining

passengers. Only two remained inside, a man and a woman, their heads pinned and locked under the buckled metal of the luggage racks. In a bus crammed with over sixty people, somehow only these two had died.

For the next half-hour the passersby walked among the strewn, groaning bodies, offering the most basic of first aid. We carried jugs of water, and we used one of Raquel's baby blankets to dab off blood. The white cloth turned red within the first few minutes. Our presence seemed almost a joke. Yet the water and the rags were welcomed by the shaking victims, as was the touch, gentle and timid, of fingers brushing away the stains. With so little to offer, we asked their names, told them ours, and talked with them. "My name is Alicia," one woman, about fifty years old, stammered. "My right eye, I can't see out of it, I can't see."

I cleaned around where her eye once was. I could not tell how deep the damage had penetrated, but tiny gnats had already collected. I called her by name, Alicia, and tried to offer calm responses.

They were everywhere. Here lay a young man whose back was twisted, and he could not feel his feet. There lay a young woman with a gash that cut through her calf to the bone. She lay and breathed deeply so as to save her pregnancy. To the side sat a whole family, a father, mother, three kids, bleeding but all alive. And here squatted a little boy with a round face and runny nose, who looked up at me. When I grinned at him, he smiled back through the screams and groans encircling us as if whatever I did, he trusted me.

We cleaned faces and arms and legs and chests for an hour and a half. No ambulance arrived. The police did, however, and their first question was, "Where is the driver?" Everyone knew that the driver had fled, for if he were caught, he immediately would have gone to jail. Never mind that the brake failure was caused by the bus line owner's refusal to have them replaced. The driver would be blamed.

It was with the arrival of the police that a ludicrous corruption unfolded. Suddenly everyone, in the presence of the cops, turned afraid to help, knowing how quickly helping could put you in jail. Other buses and cars stopped and handed out bottles of water, rubbing alcohol, rags, fruit juices. No one, however, offered a ride to a hospital, as they knew that to give rides to the victims meant being blamed if they died along the way. Yet it was almost 5:00 P.M., and the ambulances were nowhere to be seen. Only one fellow from an emergency squad showed up, wearing a fire helmet and carrying around one small box of first aid. He guided the rest of us, telling us to cut long branches to set broken bones, to cover the wounds with rags to protect them from gnats and flies. Yet he too turned angry as he waited for working companions.

A group of men formed to discuss the situation. "If we help these people," whispered one, "if we give them rides, then the police will screw us completely. This is a gold mine of bribes for them."

"Yeah, but dammit we can't just stand here, these people are dying."

The group approached one cop, who squatted beside the man with the twisted back, asking for his address, writing it down on a pad. One of the men spoke for our group. He stated that we were willing to carry people to the hospital, as long as nothing happened to us in the case of a death caused by the bus wreck. The cop almost smiled, understanding well what we all understood. "Don't worry. Nothing will happen."

Four cars lined up, and a few of the wounded were carried away. A woman named Petrona climbed into our jeep. A gash ran from the front to the back of her head. She apologized after vomiting blood a number of times out the window. For the thirty miles between the accident and the hospital Petrona shook and cried, asking God why. Driving, I trembled slightly, for I had seen the cop take down my license plate number as I pulled away.

As we entered the capital, two ambulances passed us by, their sirens screaming, heading to a two-hour-old accident.

We arrived at St. John's hospital. I half-carried Petrona through the crowds of people, relatives, newspaper photographers, children. We walked through the emergency door. Someone took her, placed her on a bed and wheeled her away. I turned, walked out, cutting through the crowds. I avoided the policemen, hopped in our jeep and fled, separating us from the scene. Michelle and Paul sat in the back with Raquel, exhausted faces hanging above their chests. Raquel cried suddenly for the first time during this long trip, as if feeling the surge of tension that washed through us like a hot breath. The accident did not leave us, and it would not, not even after we cleaned the stains off the upholstery and dashboard where Petrona had turned sick. The odor remained, that of dried crimson hanging in the air, a stagnant reminder that here, in this country, you learn to acquire a taste for death.

CHAPTER SIXTEEN

ORGANIZING

Michelle, Father Chamba, and I offered a course on land issues to the catechists. Three years had passed since such a workshop had been held here. The farmers grouped together for two days and shared their experiences of what it meant to be poor and landless. From there they planned strategies on how to deal politically with their situation.

One man sat in on the course, and nobody knew him (such workshops are given only among well-known friends). Everyone knew he was not a peasant farmer; portliness gave him away. Michelle talked to him during a coffee break, asking him about his work, his home, etc. "Oh no, I'm not a catechist. I'm a refrigerator man. I work for the Kaibiles."

Though an *ear* for the Special Forces, he was not very smart. He stared through the door during most of the meeting, obviously bored. He stared toward the military camp, as if longing for his tools and a broken icebox. The Kaibiles must not have felt very threatened by our workshop, to have sent us their repairman. We were not sure whether to feel afraid or insulted.

A group of campesinos began a protest in front of the judge's office, demanding that the judge release a couple of fellow campesinos who were unjustly thrown in jail over a land title problem. The patrón wanted their little piece of land so he could stretch his huge, many-thousand-acre farm all the way to the road. Thus, he had the boys thrown in jail.

Forty campesinos, along with Father Chamba, Michelle, and the Spanish missioner Pilar, stood in front of the courthouse and peacefully, quietly demanded to talk with the judge. He refused. After a few hours the two men were released on a lesser fine (somewhat of a win).

The following day we learned that while our friends stood outside the judge's office, the judge had called on the Kaibiles to send over a troop and gun down the crowd, "especially the priest, along with all the campesinos."

The Kaibiles decided to pay him no mind. This judge had the reputation of putting innocent people in jail so as to collect fines. He had been kicked out of other municipalities for such blatant corruption. The government had sent him to Poptún, the forgotten badlands of the nation. Here he did not create such national embarrassment. The Kaibiles knew his history, and they refused to take him seriously. Even they pick and choose their killings.

After the land workshop a number of friends asked us to help them form an inter-village committee. Such a committee would represent all the poor communities around Poptún and it would try to confront some of the common needs and problems in those areas. Public excitement kindled around the idea. Others, however, refused involvement. As one fellow yelled aloud during the meeting, "I'm not getting involved with this. This is pure subversive, pure guerrilla stuff." It seemed obvious that he said it to clean his name from the *ears* in the crowd.

Two weeks after the protest against the judge, an uprising took place in Poptún. The judge made the mistake of putting one of the market vendors in jail and forcing him to pay a high fine in order to get out. This truly was a mistake born in stupidity. The market vendors are the one link with the outside world. The Petén relies upon goods imported into the area, as the jungle was not made for communal self-sufficiency. Those who work the local stores have a unique power. You just don't mess with the market vendors.

A crowd of over 500 people stood outside of the judge's office, wielding sticks, rocks, and clubs. They yelled for him to come out peacefully, for they wanted to talk with him about his consistent use of the jail cell in order to pocket money from high fines. He did not leave the building. Rather, he and a little fellow named *Chico Pajarito* (Frankie, the little Bird), who is a Kekchi Indian and seen by both indigenous and ladinos as a serpent, boarded up the door and closed the windows. Chico Pajarito had reason to be afraid. His was the reputation of a traitor, using his native language and knowledge of his own people to extort them, translating certain data from Kekchi into Spanish for the good judge, twisting the truth into cases against them.

Some in the crowd went to the police station to demand from the Chief of Police some action. The Chief called the courthouse, but the judge cut the line. That did it. The crowd gave him ten minutes to come out. At the end of the ten minutes, they stormed the building.

The judge found himself high above the crowds, floating upon a bedding of hands. Chico Pajarito was not so lucky as to enjoy such a long journey: He too was lifted up, but tossed into a ditch. If Chico were to have looked up, he would have seen the judge drifting away, jerking about like a newborn on his back, screaming to get out of the angry crib.

The crib opened up, and the judge fell into the hole. When he appeared again, he could barely see through the blood stains over his face. Blinking his eyes, he saw that the crowd had carried him to the hospital. The hands shoved his beaten body forward. An individual stepped forward and spoke to one of the doctors.

"Fix this fucker up before we give him a taste of his own medicine."

The doctor complied, patching up the scrapes and bruises left upon the judge. Afterwards he handed the judge back over to the group.

Again they lifted him up and carried him away. The movement of people stopped in front of Suzi's, a hardware store, where they bought a huge lock. They moved straight to the police station. They entered without asking permission, and headed toward the first open cell. They coughed the judge up and spat him into the cage. Then they slammed the door and threw their newly-bought lock onto the bolt.

"You'll get out after we figure out what to do with you."

With that, the crowd moved away, dispersed, and became individuals.

Long after midnight the governor of the Petén left the state capital of Flores and quietly drove into the back of the Poptún police station. As one of his henchmen worked on the lock with a hacksaw, the governor leaned through the bars and whispered to the popularly incarcerated justice of the peace. "We're getting you out of here. You better move on, back to Guatemala City or wherever you're from."

"You mean I should leave Poptún? But I've been assigned here by the government."

"My advice is that you leave. If you stay, well, the Poptunecos, they will just kill you."

"Oh."

He left. Two days later we read in the paper about the beating the judge had received by the hands of a rowdy crowd in Poptún. The following day, an interview with the judge told the rest of the country that the poor man was a victim of the brutal, savage, jungle people of Petén who practically wear no clothes and who are constantly drugged out on cocaine. His words were destined to ratify the belief that the Petén was Guatemala's lawless land.

Other editorials surfaced in the days following, written by people who lived in other towns where this same judge had served. His history unfolded, that of arriving in a town and keeping the jails filled with people who had to pay high fines to get out. "Hooray for the *Poptunecos*," wrote one person, "for they have had the courage to stand up to extortionists such as this one and give them what they deserve."

Pilar, the Spanish missioner, smiled as she read the paper. She had been present in the weeks previous when the judge threatened to have the Kaibiles mow the crowd down. "Hah! It's about time some justice was written into this yellow rag!" I expected her to throw her chest forward and sing a Spaniard's *jota* of praise for Poptún's sudden demonstration of self-determination.

CHAPTER SEVENTEEN

ARMIES, THIEVES, AND OTHER DEVILS

According to the running voice (i.e., rumor), the guerrillas attacked the airstrip radio control tower on the runway two nights ago. A few rounds of rifle shot came from the stone hill in the neighborhood of Ixobel and rattled against the tower.

The people in Ixobel were very afraid, thinking that the army was going to show up, blaming some of their own people. According to Father Chamba, it probably was not the guerrillas that shot at the tower. "Shooting forty little shots at a metal tower? What an idiotic thought. If the guerrillas wanted to bring down such a building, they would easily strap a bomb to it and there you have it. That wasn't a guerrilla move. It probably was the army itself."

Not a surprising theory. According to the national news, the guerrillas tried to murder President Elias while he flew into the Petén on a political visit. Guerrillas usually don't work that way. Killing such a public official harms their cause. Yet it is not beyond the army to perform such theater. Since Mike DeVine's murder, the State Department in Washington cut off funds to Guatemala. The army looked for ways to get that source of dollars moving again. Shooting at the tower may have been a cheap way to get more kickbacks.

And we, living half a kilometer from the control tower, didn't hear a thing. Chico Guzmán had coffee with us and discussed the news. He had heard the gunshots from his home one mile away. He gave me a look of incredulity. "You all sleep well, don't you?"

My mother visited us during Holy Week. On Good Friday she and I walked around in the morning to partake in the festivities. Each day there was a memory-touch that raised her eyes, tossing her back into her own childhood in El Salvador.

At times the moments were not so agreeable. Michelle and I spent one evening with a youth group when the lights went out. Mom was in the house taking care of Raquel. The sudden darkness threw Mom into a little girl's terror: The machetes came down upon her father's front door, and they all ran out into the cornfield to hide for the night, while the machine guns rained down upon the Salvadoran earth. It was the beginning of a massacre that would last two weeks, taking up to 30,000 lives.

That same night, when I was driving the teenagers home (after having supper with them at a local restaurant), we passed by a street fight. Better to say a beating: a woman in her thirties slapped and punched a teenage girl in the middle of the road. The older, bigger woman pulled out a knife and threatened to kill the younger one, then started ripping the girl's hair out by the roots.

I jumped out of the jeep and yelled at her to stop. She turned one eye on me, which I could see in the moonlight. It seemed to glow red with hatred. "Get out of here gringo, and keep your prick in your own business."

I walked to my jeep, saying aloud, "Kids, should we go to the police?" I expected a positive response, but received a weak unsurety. The kids motioned for me to get in the vehicle and drive away.

Afterwards they explained why. "That's Candelina, she's the prostitute and owner of the tavern *My Kingdom*. I wouldn't call the cops on her. She keeps beds warm for all the police."

I returned home, angry and noticeably nervous over the encounter. My mother stood in the hallway, shaking under the disappeared electricity. "Where do you keep your damned candles?" She paced the house. "Sometimes I just don't understand why you want to live here," she blurted out. "It is too difficult, people shouldn't have to live like this."

My mother rarely spoke against us living abroad. Yet she knew what world we lived in, a world that once made her hide in a night-covered milpa. When the lights blew out in my house, her history invaded our present.

It rained for the first time in weeks. The storms beat mean and loud as if to inundate this mouthful of dust that we call Poptún.

Father Chamba passed through rough days. He had to walk carefully after the problems with the local judge. Before the uprising that had him tossed out of town, the judge sent a letter to the Bishop of the diocese, saying that the local priest in Poptún was "instigating the peasants" to protests and uprisings. Such words, fallen into certain hands, could mean certain death.

Chamba went to Guatemala City to get away for a few days. He pulled up to a favorite restaurant. As he got out of the car, three men surrounded him. "Give us the keys," one said. Chamba put his hands in his pockets to get them, when another ripped his pocket open. The third pulled out a gun, and the first pulled out a knife. Chamba blocked the knife with his arm before the blade would plunge into his stomach. One of the men slammed his forehead into Chamba's face. They turned to the Toyota and opened it. At that point Chamba fled, knowing that the key that opened the door was not the same key that started the engine; that one was still in his pocket. Once they tried to start it up and failed, they would be very angry. He ducked around a corner and waited until they abandoned the vehicle.

That night we too were in the city. The missioner nurse Sheila was also present. She quickly checked Chamba, looking into his eyes for signs of a concussion. During the attack the guy with the gun had brought the butt down on Chamba's head.

"How do you feel?" she asked.

"A little sore. Mostly this hand," he answered, showing her where the blade had caught him.

"You need to rest. If you're sore now, you'll really feel it tomorrow."

"That's comforting."

Three other missioners visited Chamba's room throughout the afternoon. All three of us, at one point or another, made the remark, "Tomorrow is when you'll really feel it." When Michelle mentioned this, he laughed.

"Missioners are *so* good at comforting the poor and afflicted. I just can't wait for tomorrow."

I invited him up to our room for my own rendition of medicine: a bottle of rum. Fortunately, it's one of his favorite pharmaceutical products. We drank and talked; I mostly listened as he, for the first time, poured out fears that he had locked away. In moments his machismo showed forth, saying, "I'm not afraid, I can handle it." But the attempted robbery shook him, reminding him of all the risks he'd taken for the community. I think he was appreciative of the rum, though he drank very little.

Then the rains came. The thunder and wind whipped up like an angry yet impotent god that wailed over the freedom he had bequeathed unto us.

I stayed with don Chico Guzmán's family for a week, due to the devil that had invaded his house.

Chico and his cousins were cleaning off the land with fire so as to prepare for next season's corn planting. Chico's young cousin Jorge drew too close to the fire. The flames danced out of control. Chico and his cousins fought to bring the fire back to a small size, but the flames grew as wide as three men and as tall as the tree branches.

They lost sight of Jorge. The teenager had walked into the fire. The flames surrounded him, though they did not touch him. He stumbled through an opening, mumbling half-jumbled phrases about masks in the fire. They took him back to their house in Poptún. His legs and arms quivered. At times he bolted out the door and ran into nearby fields, with Chico and his father chasing behind. They had to tie him to the bed posts.

The week passed. The family did not sleep for seven days straight. Jorge did not eat, but he kept on talking about the masks that he saw in the fire, then the giants, and the fact that, "The fire killed me and I died and then, suddenly, I was born once more."

I arrived during the week. We prayed together, as it gave them some sense of comfort. We searched for understanding in his babbling. Jorge moved his head from side to side, with his eyes opened wide yet with a strange sleepiness about them. His smile was unlike any I have ever seen, that of someone who had decided to utilize this young, pliable face, distorting it to the edge of possibilities.

Demons. Satan. Beelzebub. At night they untied Jorge to give him a rest from the bondage. He grabbed the Bible and began ripping it up. One night as they read from the Gospels, Jorge, tied once again, sucked in a great quantity of air. He released it, hurling the breath across the bed. "His breath slammed against me, don Marcos. And you know me, I am not a person to believe in these things, I'm more of the earth, of the day to day. But I swear before you, I felt a heat with that breath. An electricity shot through my shoulder and arm where he breathed on me."

Jorge spat upon them whenever they grabbed the Bible. I once stood in an adjacent room and watched as he spat toward a crucifix hanging upon the wall before him. When he talked to me, he spoke of how beautiful Michelle was. Then he laughed and fell back into mumbling about the masks in the fire.

Each day that I visited the family, I saw them sink deeper into weariness. The men worried about the mother, as she was pregnant. They were afraid of what such a presence in the house could do to the child within her. They were sure he would come into the world with numerous arms or a demon's face.

They tied Jorge to the backseat of an old car and drove him to Guatemala City. The doctor sold them brain vitamins. About the same time, Jorge began showing signs of improvement. I did not know where to give credit. Perhaps it was a deep form of heat stroke that just needed time. Or maybe it was the vitamins.

I must say that I have never felt such a presence, a fear so dark and sharp, as that within the dilapidated walls of their home. I cannot form any beliefs or theologies, nor do I want to, recognizing the futility of making sense out of such an experience. We should know our limitations.

Three weeks later I was playing guitar on the front step of my home when Jorge walked around the corner. He smiled at me. I almost snapped a string on a jerked strum. We greeted each other.

"I just came to thank you for helping me and my family last month, don Marcos. It's all gone now. He went away. He's not in me, not anymore. He's gone, and I'm thankful. I don't know if it was the vitamins or the rosaries." He talked for a long while. He remembered everything. He spoke once again of the masks in the fire, but now he did so with the sense of one who is ashamed for being the victim of abuse. Though he never said it, I knew he was practically embarrassed over the words that his voice had uttered about Michelle. "Please give doña Michelle my regards," he said before leaving my home.

We shook hands and he walked away. I never saw Jorge again, as if the fact that a devil between us would not allow for any sane friendship.

CHAPTER EIGHTEEN

UPON THE LAWLESS ROAD

René Cabrera looks like a young model from *Gentlemen's Quarterly* magazine. Thick black hair cut short, strong jaw, large dark brown eyes, and a set of teeth that would put your eyes out. He was once a seminarian, studying to become a Catholic priest. When he left the seminary, a number of young Poptunecas prayed in thanksgiving to God and the Virgin Mary that young René did not throw his good looks into the confines of celibacy.

Unfortunately for them, seminary gave René a touch of the college life. Though he left religious studies, he continued to pursue academic work in engineering. He lived most of the year in Xela, a city in western Guatemala, seventeen hours by bus from his hometown.

René came home to Poptún on an unexpected visit. Within days he would return to Xela. He passed by our house to say goodbye and to thank us for our help and support. René

smiled, though his grin was strained. He was always a gentleman, at times too good. As we listened to him, I questioned if he
could accept what had happened to him and his family, and I
wondered what he really felt about the murder of Martín Cabrera, his father.

René told the story again, recounting to Michelle and
me what we had heard through others. On Sunday afternoon
three supply trucks crawled through the Petén toward Poptún,
bringing market produce to us: vegetables, fruits, sacks of corn
and beans, boxes of canned processed food, cheese, powdered
milk. Eight men were divided among the trucks, and they traveled
together for protection, as robbery had been a common practice
recently. The one road through the state had seen several attacks.
Hidden men in the jungle had been waiting for trucks such as
these.

Martín Cabrera, the driver of the first truck, drove
ahead upon the stony Petén road. The two thieves came out of
the jungle and took advantage of a muddy, precarious incline
where Martín had to gear down. They forced him down from
the truck, put a bullet between his eyes and into his chest,
dragged him to the edge of the road, and dumped him in the
woods. Then they took the truck, along with Martín's young
helper, drove it a little further up the road, and waited for the
other two vehicles of the convoy. When they were finished seven
were dead, one of them a fourteen-year-old boy.

When René came home from Xela, his neighbors had
already formed search parties for his father, the only missing
person. They spent all Monday and Tuesday looking for him.
After forty-eight hours of walking through the jungle, yelling
out his name, asking people in nearby villages, then coming

home at night to offer no news to waiting wives, it was a dark relief to find his remains. In the gamut of violences, death is much more acceptable than disappearance.

René drank a cup of coffee at our house. He absent-mindedly played with Raquel. Our daughter, like every other young lady in town, smiled shyly at him. René spoke of the practicalities that followed the tragedy, the fact that his father had taken this truck driving job in order to put him through college. "He just wanted to see me finish. I'd be the first person in my neighborhood to make it through school. Now I need to find other means of payment, or else return home."

"I have an idea. Xela is famous for its leather goods, especially shoes. I'm thinking of buying shoes there, then bringing them here to Poptún and sell them. I think that could be a little profitable. People want good shoes."

We took a retreat in Antigua, the small old colonial town south of Guatemala City. It came at an appropriate time. Many of us left Poptún together, feeling strength in numbers. The robberies and murders on the jungle road had increased since the time of Martín Cabrera's death. Once we hit the asphalt road, we geared into fifth and shook off anxiety like kicked up dust.

In Antigua, we stayed in the Posada Belén, now famous for being the site where Sister Dianna Ortíz had disappeared.

I was to return alone to Poptún for a few days. Michelle had meetings in the city, and meetings were also planned back home. Splitting up was necessary. Yet if I were to step back, I had to question our decisions. Too much bad had happened in too little time. The thieves took advantage of the rain that slowed down traffic. People we knew had been killed on that overused road. The spastic rants of the judge still echoed through the streets of Poptún, along with his threat to have the Kaibiles mow our people down. Father Chamba still limped carefully through his days as he convalesced from his knife wounds.

We made our decisions. Old Brother Leon and I were to leave together early in the morning. I would return by bus two days later. Soon after that, Michelle, Raquel, and I would fly to the United States for a vacation with our families.

I packed a small bag. Late that evening, while Raquel slept on her cot, Michelle and I made love. The night turned, you could say, rapacious. I was surprised we did not wake our girl up. Yet we touched as if it were our last opportunity to do so.

Brother Leon and I drove along the rocky Petén road toward Poptún. It had begun as a pleasant trip, as pleasant as this road could possibly be. Leon was always good company, and if you prodded him, he played familiar tunes on his harmonica.

I drove along at a good clip until we arrived at the back end of a parked gas tank truck. A line of trucks, jeeps, and buses covered the rolling hills before us. Beyond them stood other parked vehicles, but they faced us.

It did not look hopeful. I left Brother Leon with his harmonica, a loaf of bread, and a jar of peanut butter. "Don't eat all that while I'm gone," I said. "Looks like we'll need it." I ran down to see the culprit of all this stopped traffic. In the middle of the two facing lines a beer truck nested halfway into a one-lane bridge. The truck's back wheels had splintered through several planks and had lodged themselves between the iron rods under the bridge. Below its rear end a deep river rushed by.

Men gathered round both ends of the bridge. They formed groups of grumbling, cigarette-smoke ideas. They had already tried to jack the truck onto the planks. Three men had wrestled with the jack, balancing it upon the lower beams. The final recourse slowly made its way into the group: Empty the truck of its beer, lighten the load, then pull the truck out.

We formed lines and began tossing cases of *Gallo Cerveza*, Rooster Beer, to one another. After thirty minutes of swinging and catching, the truck was half-empty. "Let's give it a go," smiled the heavy-set truck driver. He tossed a cable from the front of his crippled vehicle to another truck on land. The other driver hooked up the cable while the beer man climbed onto his seat. While they worked quietly, a hunched-over elderly gentle-man with no shoes and a holey straw hat stood near me and mumbled, "It's not going to work, you're going to make things worse."

His mutterings were lost in the fervor of an almost com-pleted mission. The men smiled as they looked at the setup. They smacked the sides of the wrecker truck as it revved up to save the day. Nothing was heard but the roar of two motors as the cable pulled taut.

The beer truck did not pop up onto the bridge and roll away. The four back wheels that sank through the bridge acted as giant fish hooks. As the cable pulled tight, those wheels snagged deep into the planks and pulled the bridge right along with them. Two-by-sixes flew upward, snapping like three dozen toothpicks under a hatchet blade.

The dust settled. The wood rubble fell to either side. Some planks dropped to the river and washed downstream, escaping our sight. The beer truck sat on a pile of collapsed wood like some huge metal chicken that had come to roost. Over to one side I heard the old man mumbling in Spanish, "I told you, I told you. Dangit."

Old Brother Leon walked up from our Toyota. His hands on his hips and the harmonica sticking out of one hand, he approached the edge of the cliff and looked through the bridge's brand new gaping hole that displayed the river's deep rush.

"Problems?" he asked.

Plan two: Reconstruct the bridge. Unfortunately, no one carried any ten-inch nails, so we simply placed the planks one next to the other, right on top of the iron beams. The men—most of them truck drivers—worked quickly and effi-ciently. They tossed lassos from one bank to the other, dragged planks across the beams, and balanced themselves on the beam edges, all the while making editorial comments on the national situation. ("This is the *chingado* work of Vinicio, promising us the world as president, then leaving us high and dry, yep, Vinicio and those *jodidos* who do the road work, they do nothing but sit on their *vergas* all day long, all those *pendejos* do is put us poor *chapínes encachimbados*, having to fix *chingado* bridges like this one, *al carajo* with the whole lot of them.")

With the planks down, we had one more job to do: put the beer back on the truck. We became more efficient with our beer-slinging. We formed one long line from the pile of cases to the back of the truck. Not one case touched the ground. We flung them to one another, swiveling our hips in one clean motion, all of us synchronized with one another's movements. We laughed and talked as we worked, and among strangers a camaraderie formed. Jokes were tossed along with beer cases. ("Hey, let's toss a few of these babies into the weeds for afterwards. We got this gringo working like a *chapín*. Let's see if he can drink like one too!")

When the beer was repacked, the truck pulled away. Every vehicle motor on the face of the earth turned over, and the jungle hills filled with the snarls of two miles of frustrated drivers. "We better get goin'!" yelled Leon.

We ran to the Toyota and pulled up ahead. I watched the bridge as gigantic eighteen-wheelers pulled over it, filled to the brim with illegally-cut mahogany. The bridge bent and crackled, bulging toward the river below like a stiff rubber band. A truck driver yelled to me from his seat, "Go on ahead!" He let me pass. Our little Toyota truck on the bridge was a relief to the rotting planks.

We drove over. I released a heavy breath of fatigue and thanksgiving. "That was somethin', wasn't it?" mumbled Leon. He pulled out his harmonica, and played me a Willie Nelson tune about blue eyes, how they wept in the rain upon parting from one's lover.

I pushed it into third, closing the gap between us and Poptún. I hoped to see my family in two days, though this bridge had made that a precarious desire.

Leon finished his song, then looked at me with a side glance and a chuckle. "Hey, how about another love song? Oops. Guess not."

After the meeting with all the ministerial groups in the morning, Chico Guzmán and I went by old don Pablo's house for coffee and sweet bread.

Don Pablo took us out back to show us his garden. He is in his sixties, with a sinewy frame, hair white as clouds and a matching moustache that curls into perfect handlebars. "So you and doña Michelle are going to the States for vacation? You better be careful. If you're there longer than you're supposed to be, Chico and I will have to hit the road north and drag your tail back here."

I put my head down and smiled humbly, yet thankful for the compliment. "Don't you worry, don Pablo. Before you know it we'll be back, drinking all your coffee and chewing your ear off."

"Hah! You better be careful. You got a mother-in-law? Well, she may just grab you this time around and not let you get on that plane. Or your mother herself. I've met doña Amanda, Marquitos. She could get ahold of you too."

The afternoon passed. I returned to the parish house and found Chamba behind a typewriter. "You ready for your vacation?" he smiled. "How about some chapína food before you hit the road?"

He had mass at 7:00 o'clock in the evening. Afterwards we drove by Pilar Martín's house on the way to supper to see if she would be interested. She greeted us at the door with Pilar-kisses and an energetic welcome. "Oh, no, I cannot go with you. I've got an appointment over at the Center. But I've got time for a moment of levity, hah! Sit down, sit down," and she opened up the hammock before disappearing into the outside kitchen and finding a half-full bottle of Spanish wine. Chamba swung in the hammock. I leaned back in a chair. A night of relaxation had begun.

We left Pilar's house ("You tell that Raquelita that I'll be waiting for her in August, and that I'll have no mercy when we play together again") and went over to a restaurant named "La Chapina" at 8:30. La Chapina offers small booths for each party. Built like a hut, three or four people can sit comfortably under the thatched roof. Privacy was somewhat secured by the bamboo walls around us. We still lowered our voices whenever we referred to certain entities: army, landowners, death squads, and the women Father Chamba thought about.

We ordered a bottle of rum and two soft drinks: a Coke and a Seven-Up. "Let me teach you something very important, Marcos. Perhaps I have revealed this secret to you before (he had, several times). You take rum and pour it over the ice, thusly. Then you poor just enough Coke into it, then just enough Seven-Up. You see, the Coke raises the strength of the rum, the Seven-Up lowers it. In this manner you create the perfect equilibrium." He smiled and raised his glass. "Here's to equilibrium."

He pulled a pack of cigarettes from his pocket and tossed them upon the table. We sat, smoked, drank, conversed about all that was important and secondary. At some point in the night we got around to eating. He spoke about the situation with the teachers in the villages, how they never showed up, leaving the village people without access to education. "I got an audience with the Minister of Education in Guatemala City. It was tremendous. You usually can only get ten minutes with her, but we spoke with her for almost an hour. She's coming to the Petén in July. The first time a Minister of Education will visit the Peten. Things are moving, Marquitos. Here's to movement."

We toasted. The conversation opened doors to certain inner questions. Chamba said, "I was talking with Chepe Valle the other day, you know, the teacher over at the high school. We were discussing the arrival of the Minister. Suddenly he looked up at me and asked, 'Why do you keep moving, Chamba?' I wasn't sure what he meant. He said, 'You just keep on going, keep on getting involved. Why?' You know, it was the first time that was asked of me. It was the first time I asked myself. I couldn't answer him. For the first time in a long while, I had nothing to say." He dragged from his cigarette. "I don't know. Maybe it has to do with the deaths of my parents. Or my aunt, who was gang raped. I'm not sure. It's a good question. Maybe someday I'll have an answer for it. But I guess I'll keep moving. Until somebody stops me. And then, I'll move stronger than ever." He laughed and held his glass in front of his eyes.

We got into other subjects, everything from martyrdom to celibacy to sexuality. Such conversations happen inevitably in this very Chapín liturgy of cigarettes, rum, beans, tortillas, friendship.

We ate supper at about 10:00. It began to rain. An hour later Chamba took me to the bus stop. He shook my hand goodbye. "Say hello to doña Amanda for me. Tell her I hope to see her again soon." I wished him well with the Minister of Education, and told him I looked forward to seeing him in a month. I walked into the bus office. Chamba went home to bed.

I sat, waiting for the bus. This had been the trip that I had dreaded all weekend. Eight hours later the sun would rise. I would walk into the missionary house in the capital, go upstairs, and kiss my wife good morning. I only had to get this lawless road out from under me.

The Maya Express pulled out of Poptún only half an hour late. By midnight I was asleep, in as much of a dream as the rocky road allowed. The Maya—a new set of buses that had yet to lose parts to the crude stones of Petén trips—geared into fourth along some stretches and grinded its way through the mountains. I woke up only when the bus braked somewhere between pitch darkness and nowhere. Our headlights shined against the back of a lumber truck. We waited. A few ventured out, and in a few minutes they returned. "It's a bridge, about a kilometer up ahead. A soda truck went through it. From here to the bridge is parked traffic."

It was the same bridge I had helped reconstruct about forty-eight hours ago. Everyone in the bus groaned in unison, as if acquiescing to our approaching communal nightmare.

"Nothing to do but sit and wait, see what happens," muttered our bus driver as he flipped off all the lights. He pulled a baseball cap over his eyes. Above us heat lightning grumbled through the sky, displaying the tops of jungle trees. Between lightning shots, pure darkness enveloped us. I heard only a few careful whispers, "Are you asleep? No, I'm not asleep. You? No way, I'm not sleeping. There are guerrillas out here, you know.

And thieves. Did you hear about the seven men murdered near here just two weeks ago? Yeah. And there are animals too. Jungle cats. And snakes. I'm not sleeping. No way."

We all stayed awake for the next hour and a half, then jumped to the voice outside that yelled, "Maya Express! The other Maya from Guatemala City is here, on the other side of the bridge. Time to switch passengers."

I grabbed my small bag and walked with other passengers toward the bridge. I calculated how late I would arrive. Two hours was not so bad, Michelle would not worry too much. Yet it would take at least an hour to switch passengers plus all their luggage strapped on top of both buses. The bridge also stood in the way. It was now 3:30 A.M. With lightning shattering all around us and a drizzle of rain collecting on our faces, along with the rush of muddy river water roaring far below, the ambience had changed. I expected Indiana Jones to come swinging out of a tree to save the day, especially as I stared through all the holes in the bridge. "Here," said one worker of the Maya Express, "we put down some planks for you all to walk on. Just lean toward the truck, but don't lean *too* hard."

We moved one at a time, stepping on slick planks. A two-by-six slipped over from the weight of a portly fellow in front of me. I stopped breathing. The plank tumbled back in place. I crossed over, then looked back at the broken wood, the other people moving, and the soda truck whose back tires had fallen through the bridge. Hollywood could not have done it better.

We loaded up in our new bus. The driver adroitly pulled it around, turned it, and squeezed by the long line of stopped vehicles. We all applauded him.

Two hours later the bus lurched to another stop. The driver shut down the lights once again, kicked back, lowered the baseball cap. Another line of vehicles stood before us. "Bridge is out. Carried away by the river," informed someone through the window to the chauffeur. A groan, like a muffled Gregorian chant, rose from us all. Nothing to do but wait until the river went down.

Dawn came to the jungle. I would have appreciated such a moment were I not so sticky with old sweat and morning breath. A few of us left the bus. We stared hard at the river so as to intimidate it into lowering more quickly.

Three hours passed before a bus in front of us dared to plough through the water. He made it. The dare was on. The passengers all looked at our driver with "Well?" in their eyes.

"I'll try in a minute. Just let me smoke my cigarette."

He smoked slowly. He lit another one from the butt of the first. He had seen the first bus that had looked ready to float over to one side when it tried. Our boy finished his fag, dropped it to the ground and turned to his machine. "Here we go."

He ploughed through. We all crossed the one skinny plank left from the bridge and scrambled onto the Maya. It was 9:00 A.M. when we left the scene. It took ten hours to get through to Petén, a trip that is usually four hours long. We had five more hours of asphalt before us. No chance of calling Michelle.

We arrived at 2:00 P.M. A taxi driver stood nearby, a friendly fellow who knew the quickest way to the Center House. I paid, jumped out of the car, and I could not run quickly enough to the door. I fumbled with the keys and plunged through the door to the lobby where Michelle had also run, her eyes welling up with worry that had intensified with every hour that I was late, here, in a country where to be late can mean too many things. We embraced. Raquel put an arm on my shoulder. She looked back and forth at each of us. The worry that had filled Michelle from her stomach to her throat now receded with a wash of tears. We held onto one another, a family longing to close up distances.

CHAPTER NINETEEN

DESPEDIDAS

In the States we learned about Pilar Martín Perez's death. The phone call came to my parents' house. Pilar had been driving the road from Poptún to Flores, the capital of the Petén. She passed a slow moving bus on the dusty, rock road, just as a man wandered in front of her jeep. The fellow, it was later learned, was mentally handicapped. He was known by the folks of his village to wander in front of moving vehicles. Pilar swerved to the left to miss both the man and the bus. She also hit the brakes. The jeep flipped over twice before flinging her passengers out. Pilar was caught underneath the metal. It crushed her skull.

She lived for a few days. The hemorrhage was too great, and she died in Guatemala City.

Though we were in the States with family, the vacation suddenly twisted into entrapment. The need to be in Poptún now closed upon us.

I pictured Poptún, sitting in a silence that was too still, waiting for festivities that never came. Waiting for that beautiful woman to stand up before the crowd and jut forward one shoulder, with her hands on her waist, while a song of *jota* burst forth like a sensual thunderstorm, wet and rambunctious.

Pilar, may you always sing.

I have always been a maladroit when it comes to *despedidas*, or saying goodbye. Now I walk about in the debris of memories. I remember those final moments as an itinerant stone kicker, acting like a photographer without a camera, with only a pen and a sheet of paper soaking in tears and laughter. I remember when I first went there, to that country, when the people greeted me with a "May God bless you, Mister Gringo." Then I left, taking with me a gift of memory, of faces of people who stooped over to kiss the earth, of hands that snatched up tortillas and beans, of eyes that wetted in a final goodbye, and the smiles that dared to say, "Oh, Marquitos, may God bless you, child."

I now wake up to cool mornings. I fix coffee in an electric percolator. I sit in front of a computer, banging out thoughts and words, trying to write myself out of the whipped up wind of confusion. The sun rises, and I look through a window (made of glass) to see a Honda Civic, our car. Outside, there is the noticeable absence of any army. I drink water from the tap, not having to boil it. The radio and television speak English. The streets are paved. The trees are naked, shedding their final clothes of autumn, standing shy in winter.

The rest of the family rises. Raquel stands at the door of her own bedroom, staring defiantly at the plastic fence that keeps her in. Michelle walks to the bathroom, gently rubbing the stretched skin of her abdomen, sending the first morning messages to the person inside. Six months pregnant now, and she walks in beauty. Sometimes Raquel and I put our faces to Michelle's stomach to talk or laugh at the little one. Once he/she kicked me square in the nose (a sign of things to come?). Within the whirlwind of change, this pregnancy is joy. I, as a father, am cautiously happy.

We learned of the pregnancy while visiting family in the States. Happiness came with the news, though it was not free of other realities, ones which the doctor warned us of. There had been slight bleeding, similar to that of our past miscarriages. The doctor suggested that we not go back overseas. Such a trip could put the pregnancy at risk.

Undesired decisions were made. My mother and I returned to Poptún to collect our belongings and to say goodbye. My brother made a tape of Michelle saying her despedida to the folks. I showed it to the two adult education groups we had worked with. I also hauled a television and a VCR to a number of barrios who requested to see the tape. It was effective, touching off a tear here and there. People were willing to speak before a videocam and do the same, saying final words to Michelle from a land where formal goodbyes are necessary for healing.

I spent the days with don Chico and the evenings with Father Chamba. Chico and I visited a number of nearby villages plus the barrios. Mom sometimes went along, though she was good to give me room to hang out with friends for a final time. She also wanted to hook up with some ladies she knew and go shopping. Some days I would be riding my bike down the street and see Mom with a small group of women, all of them heading to the market.

Chico and I visited the home of don Pablo and doña Roselia. The old man laughed and eyed me. "I told you so. You remember what I said the last time you came here, before your vacation?"

"Yes, don Pablo, but you said my mother-in-law would have something to do with us leaving."

"Hah! No doubt she did! You never know what a person prays, or whose prayer is stronger."

At night, after meetings or mass, Chamba and I hung out. We went to a restaurant or to a room in the parish house and talked through the evenings, always with cigarettes, rum, Coke and Seven-Up in hand.

"Have I ever told you about the equilibrium between the two sodas, and their effect on the levity of rum?"

"Yes, I believe so, but please, remind me."

We ate supper about 11:00 every night. Nothing is quite so rich as unplanned decadence among friends.

Chamba was disappointed about our departure. He was sad, as we had created a friendship. But perhaps more so, he was frustrated, knowing that some of the pastoral work would not be finished. The groups that we worked with would change, perhaps slow down for awhile. I felt dead guilty about this, though I knew that life would go on here, and people would find their own destinies with or without the presence of missioners. For the moment I tried to forget about such questions over the relevancy of missioners in others' countries. So did Chamba. Our *despedida* was a quicksilver moment. It was slipping away, and we dove deep to enjoy it.

Chico helped pack up the jeep with our belongings. The evening before I had videotaped him saying goodbye to Michelle. It was not until that moment that he lowered his head. "God, it's hard, it's just too hard, to make friends, then to say goodbye to them. . . . First Pilar's death, and now, your departure. . . . At least there is a certain beauty in your leaving, no? Pilar left with death, you and Michelle leave with life. You need to care for that new life."

After almost half an hour he composed himself. "All right, don Marcos, I think I'm ready." He looked into the camera, and gave a formal and warm address to Michelle, wishing her well, may God bless her and the little one inside, "and many thanks for your presence here with us, and most especially, your friendship."

We packed the jeep together. A number of people came around the vehicle. We exchanged final embraces. Mom and I climbed in. Chamba slapped my arm and smiled. "We'll see you again, don't you worry. Hey, give them hell in the States. Lots going on there too, you know." I looked down, grabbed my sunglasses, and hid behind them.

We drove away. I honked my horn to houses and to people on the road. I drove slowly, then pulled around a corner that passed by our home. I kicked it into third and took the long road around the army's runway, the stretch of dust that carried me away from the flat town and its little mountain in the center, with the three crosses that stood as a welcome and a final wave. I became yet another individual in a long history of missioners, the people who always come, then always go away. It was then that water fell from under my sunglasses. I cried useless tears. My mother held my hand as I muttered incoherent phrases of impotency.

In the airport I wrote a few lines to Miguel Angel Asturias. I wrote them in his book titled *Hombres de Maíz*, "The Corn Men." I thought I could use the lines someday in a poem. For now I just wrote them to the novelist himself.

Asturias' work, which won him the Nobel Prize for Literature, is difficult. It is based in rich Guatemalan folklore, myths, and Maya histories. Yet I suppose reading his work is no more different than learning to live in his country as an outsider, and finding that, in the midst of all the pain and the haunting presence of armies, demons, and death, there always remains an *abrazo* somewhere nearby, there always stand Guatemalans who dare to trust you as an outsider, who desire to be a friend.

> I stand here, don Miguel, in an airport that separates me from the dark women who walk on leather feet, and who slap tortillas until the sun falls into the frying pan.
>
> I was in your land for a short while, getting to know the corn man's life, touching a few people, risking friendships, watching as *chapines* risked friendships with me.

While writing, my eyes turned wet. I cursed myself for not having the power of Joyce, to stand at a distance, to file my fingernails as the world walked by my pen. A woman spoke over a speaker, announcing our flight. Women and men stood around a coffee table and talked about Guatemalan colors, how cheap they are to buy; they talked about those simple little Indian people, how cute, how passive. They spoke, and the woman on the speaker beckoned my mother and me to our flight, and the jet geared up its engines. I wrote quickly, as if to fling a lasso to this country.

Allow me to read you, don Miguel. Let me take your books with me. Guide me through the words and the paragraphs, through the colors, the men stooped over with machete in hand, the women who make tortillas out of sunlight. Thus, perhaps I can somehow return to your soul-pricking country, Guatemala.

EPILOGUE

Michelle and I walked upstairs to the upper bedroom in our apartment. We kissed Raquel goodnight and handed her over to my parents for the evening. A few hours later the midwife arrived. We worked all through the night, Michelle exerting the most energy. Heather, the midwife, listened to the whisperings of birth, discerning quickly and adroitly which stages had passed, which were still to come.

A strength drove through Michelle, one that originated from some deep, cracked sanctum. It released itself through her body, escaping like a spirit in her exhaled war with life. In the upper bedroom of our apartment a second daughter was born to us. Emily Jean came to the world healthy. My mother exclaimed, "It is a triumph indeed!"

We watched slides of our life in Guatemala. It tugged at us, sometimes crudely. The *cerro*, that large hill in the middle of town, with the three crosses atop it, flashed up against our apartment wall.

"Who knows," said Michelle, "they said that the person who climbs the mound is destined to return to the Petén."

Raquel climbed up into my lap, blatantly hinting that it was bedtime. She rested her head in the crux of my arm. I pushed my fingers through her thick hair and flipped a few more times through the slides. There stood Chico, smiling through the stalks of la milpa, carrying a small load of wood to build a corn-roasting fire. Another shot was of don Pablo, laughing at the photographer. Oli held up Raquel while leaning against her door. Pilar flashed a Hollywood smile at the camera. Father Chamba stared ahead, daring the world to bring on a fight.

We watched the slides a couple of evenings, then put them away in a closet, as if it were possible to box away histories.

It took a few years to return to the notes and journals that I had kept while living in Guatemala. As a writer I turned to other subjects. Yet the piles of notes, along with books, magazines, and newspaper clippings stood forever in a corner of a bookshelf in my office.

One morning as I wrote this manuscript, my daughters came to visit. They chatted and fought together in both English and Spanish. While Emily found one corner to play in, Raquel found another.

Knowing that Daddy was busy writing, Raquel decided

to rearrange that same pile of memories from the bookshelf. She placed all the books on the floor in a row like a bridge. One book stood out in her sight, Jean-Marie Simon's *Guatemala: Eternal Spring, Eternal Tyranny*.

Raquel sat down and flipped slowly through the pages of the photo book. Her eyes gazed at the colorful pictures of the people and land. "Ooh, *bonito*, pretty!" she said, whenever looking at the familiar multicolors of a woman's *huipil* (dress). "Oh no. Daddy? She has an owie?" asked Raquel as she pointed to a photo of a woman's tortured cadaver.

I left my desk, leaned down, and frowned at the photo. "Yes, she has an owie." I turned the page toward other photos. "Look at that. A Milpa. See that? It's corn. *Maíz*."

Raquel repeated the word in both her languages. She looked at the people who walked in front of the milpa. Women in indigenous dress walked away from the cornfield after a long day of work. Children scooted beside them.

"They working?" asked Raquel.

"Working hard," I smiled. "Now they're going home to rest."

"In their houses?"

"Yep. In their houses. In Guatemala."

"GUA-TE-MA-LA!" announced Raquel proudly, pronouncing perfectly the one multisyllabic word she knows. She said it again and again. Her sister Emily joined the chant. They danced about that pile of memories in the corner of my office, the photos and news reports and human rights documents and affidavits of the dead and disappeared. Their little girls' voices sang the word in an innocent lilt, Guatemala, Guatemala, Guatemala.

COLOPHON

Marcos McPeek Villatoro is a "Latino Southerner," with roots in El Salvador and the Appalachian Mountains. A lecturer, artist, and storyteller, he's also written the novel, *A Fire in the Earth*, and several articles for national magazines. He lives in Oneonta, Alabama.

The text was set in Minion, a typeface designed by Roger Slimbach. The display face is Lithos designed by Carol Twombly. The spot art is a font designed by Michelle Dixon called Pre-Columbian Ornaments One.

This book was typeset by Alabama Book Composition, Deatsville, Alabama.

The book was printed by Thomson-Shore, Inc., Dexter, Michigan on acid free paper.